MW01169795

Contents

Tzatziki

Yield: Approximately 2 cups

Tzatziki is a classic Greek sauce made out of strained yogurt and cucumber, and can be enjoyed as a dip for raw vegetables, or dolloped over grilled meat of your choice.

Ingredients:

- 1 (12-ounce) cucumber, peeled, halved along the length, seeded, and shredded
- 1 cup whole-milk Greek yogurt
- 1 small garlic clove, minced
- 2 tablespoons extra-virgin olive oil
- 2 tablespoons minced fresh mint and/or dill
- Salt and pepper

Directions:

1. Toss cucumber with ½ teaspoon salt using a colander and allow to drain for about fifteen minutes.
2. Beat yogurt, oil, mint, and garlic together in a container, then combine in the drained cucumber. Cover and put in the fridge until chilled, minimum sixty minutes or up to 2 days. Drizzle with salt and pepper to taste before you serve.

Bonus: Soups

Soups go well before a big meal. Go ahead and try these delicious and nutritious soups!

Artichoke-Mushroom Soup

Yield: 4 to 6 Servings

Artichokes, mushrooms, and root vegetables taste great together in s soup!

Ingredients:

- ¼ cup dry white wine
- ¼ cup heavy cream
- 1 leek, white and light green parts only, halved along the length, sliced ¼ inch thick, and washed thoroughly
- 1 teaspoon minced fresh thyme or ¼ teaspoon dried
- 1 teaspoon white wine vinegar, plus extra for seasoning
- 12 ounces white mushrooms, trimmed and sliced thin
- 2 anchovy fillets, rinsed, patted dry, and minced
- 2 bay leaves
- 2 tablespoons minced fresh tarragon
- 3 cups chicken broth
- 3 cups jarred whole baby artichokes packed in water, quartered, rinsed, and patted dry
- 3 cups vegetable broth
- 3 tablespoons all-purpose flour

- 3 tablespoons extra-virgin olive oil
- 4 garlic cloves, minced
- 6 ounces parsnips, peeled and cut into ½-inch pieces
- Salt and pepper

Directions:

1. Heat 1 tablespoon oil in Dutch oven on moderate heat until it starts to shimmer. Put in artichokes and cook until browned, eight to ten minutes. Move to slicing board, allow to cool slightly, then chop coarse.
2. Heat 1 tablespoon oil in now-empty pot on moderate heat until it starts to shimmer. Put in mushrooms, cover, and cook until they have released their liquid, approximately five minutes. Uncover and carry on cooking until mushrooms are dry, approximately five minutes.
3. Mix in leek and residual 1 tablespoon oil and cook until leek is softened and mushrooms become browned, eight to ten minutes. Mix in garlic, anchovies, and thyme and cook until aromatic, approximately half a minute. Mix in flour and cook for about sixty seconds. Mix in wine, scraping up any browned bits, and cook until nearly evaporated, about 1 minute.
4. Slowly beat in chicken broth and vegetable broth, smoothing out any lumps. Mix in artichokes, parsnips, and bay leaves and bring to simmer. Decrease heat to low, cover, and simmer gently until parsnips are tender, fifteen to twenty minutes. Remove from the heat, discard bay leaves. Mix in cream, tarragon, and vinegar. Drizzle with salt, pepper, and extra vinegar to taste. Serve.

Classic Chicken Broth

Yield: Approximately 8 cups

Chicken broth is a timeless classic, almost all over the planet.

Ingredients:

- 1 onion, chopped
- 14 cups water
- 2 bay leaves
- 2 teaspoons salt
- 4 pounds chicken backs and wings

Directions:

1. Heat chicken and water in big stockpot or Dutch oven on moderate to high heat until boiling, skimming off any scum that comes to surface. Decrease heat to low and simmer slowly for three hours.
2. Put in onion, bay leaves, and salt and continue to simmer for another 2 hours.
3. Strain broth through fine-mesh strainer into a big container, pressing on solids to extract as much liquid as possible. Allow broth to settle for approximately five minutes, then skim off fat. (Cooled broth will keep safely in a fridge for maximum 4 days or frozen for maximum 1 month.)

Classic Croutons

Yield: Approximately 3 cups

Got some stale bread lying around you want to get rid of? This recipe will get the job done.

Ingredients:

- 3 tablespoons extra-virgin olive oil
- 6 slices hearty white sandwich bread, crusts removed, cut into ½-inch cubes (3 cups)
- Salt and pepper

Directions:

1. Place the oven rack in the centre of the oven and pre-heat your oven to 350 degrees. Toss bread with oil, sprinkle with salt and pepper, and spread in rimmed baking sheet. Bake until a golden brown colour is achieved and it becomes crunchy, 20 minutes to half an hour, stirring halfway through baking.
2. Allow it to cool and serve. (Croutons can be stored safely at room temperature for up to 3 days.)

Classic Gazpacho

Yield: 8 to 10 Servings

A refreshing cold chilli tomato soup popular in southern Spain!

Ingredients:

- ⅓ cup sherry vinegar
- ½ small sweet onion or 2 large shallots, chopped fine
- 1 teaspoon hot sauce (optional)
- 1½ pounds tomatoes, cored and cut into ¼-inch pieces
- 2 garlic cloves, minced
- 2 red bell peppers, stemmed, seeded, and cut into ¼-inch pieces
- 2 small cucumbers (1 peeled, both sliced along the length, seeded, and cut into ¼-inch pieces)
- 5 cups tomato juice
- 8 ice cubes
- Extra-virgin olive oil
- Salt and pepper

Directions:

1. Mix tomatoes, bell peppers, cucumbers, onion, vinegar, garlic, and 2 teaspoons salt in a big container (at least 4-quart) and season with pepper to taste. Allow to stand until vegetables barely start to discharge their juices, approximately five minutes. Mix in tomato juice, ice cubes, and hot sauce, if using. Cover and put in the fridge to blend flavours, minimum 4 hours or for maximum 2 days.
2. Scoop out and throw away any ice cubes that remain, and sprinkle soup with salt and pepper to taste. Pour into your soup bowls, drizzle with oil, and serve.

Cold Cucumber-Yogurt Soup

Yield: 6 Servings

A fresh-tasting chilled soup popular in Turkey and Greece.

Ingredients:

- ¼ teaspoon sugar
- 1 tablespoon lemon juice
- 1½ tablespoons minced fresh dill
- 1½ tablespoons minced fresh mint
- 2 cups plain Greek yogurt
- 2 cups water
- 4 scallions, green parts only, chopped coarse
- 5 pounds English cucumbers, peeled and seeded (1 cucumber cut into ½-inch pieces, remaining cucumbers cut into 2-inch pieces)
- Extra-virgin olive oil
- Salt and pepper

Directions:

1. Toss 2-inch pieces of cucumber with scallions. Working in 2 batches, process cucumber-scallion mixture using a blender with water until smoothened thoroughly, approximately two minutes; move to big container. Beat in yogurt, lemon juice, 1½ teaspoons salt, sugar, and pinch pepper. Cover and put in the fridge to combine the flavours, minimum sixty minutes or maximum 12 hours.
2. Mix in dill and mint and sprinkle with salt and pepper to taste. Serve, topped with remaining ½-inch pieces of cucumber and drizzled with oil.

Fiery Moroccan Chicken Lentil Soup

Yield: 8 Servings

Ingredients:

- ¼ cup harissa, plus extra for serving
- ¼ teaspoon cayenne pepper
- ¼ teaspoon ground cinnamon
- ⅓ cup minced fresh cilantro
- ½ teaspoon paprika
- ¾ cup green or brown lentils, picked over and rinsed
- 1 (15-ounce) can chickpeas, rinsed
- 1 onion, chopped fine
- 1 tablespoon all-purpose flour
- 1 tablespoon extra-virgin olive oil
- 1 teaspoon grated fresh ginger
- 1 teaspoon ground cumin
- 10 cups chicken broth

- 1½ pounds bone-in split chicken breasts, trimmed
- 4 plum tomatoes, cored and cut into ¾-inch pieces
- Pinch saffron threads, crumbled
- Salt and pepper

Directions:

1. Pat chicken dry using paper towels and sprinkle with salt and pepper. Heat oil in Dutch oven on moderate to high heat until just smoking. Brown chicken lightly, approximately three minutes each side; move to plate.
2. Put in onion to fat left in pot and cook on moderate heat till they become tender, approximately five minutes. Mix in ginger, cumin, paprika, cinnamon, cayenne, ¼ teaspoon pepper, and saffron and cook until aromatic, approximately half a minute. Mix in flour and cook for about sixty seconds. Slowly beat in broth, scraping up any browned bits and smoothing out any lumps, and bring to boil.
3. Mix in lentils and chickpeas, then nestle chicken into pot and bring to simmer. Cover, decrease the heat to low, and simmer gently until chicken registers 160 degrees, fifteen to twenty minutes.
4. Move chicken to slicing board, allow to cool slightly, then shred into bite-size pieces using 2 forks, discarding skin and bones. In the meantime, continue to simmer lentils, covered, for 25 to 30 minutes.
5. Mix in shredded chicken and cook until heated through, approximately two minutes. Mix in tomatoes, cilantro, and harissa and sprinkle with salt and pepper to taste. Serve, passing extra harissa separately.

French Lentil Soup

Yield: 4 to 6 Servings

Ingredients:

- ½ cup dry white wine
- 1 (14.5-ounce) can diced tomatoes, drained
- 1 bay leaf
- 1 cup lentilles du Puy, picked over and rinsed
- 1 large onion, chopped fine
- 1 teaspoon minced fresh thyme or ¼ teaspoon dried
- 1½ cups water
- 1½ teaspoons balsamic vinegar
- 2 carrots, peeled and chopped
- 3 garlic cloves, minced
- 3 slices bacon, cut into ¼-inch pieces
- 3 tablespoons minced fresh parsley
- 4½ cups chicken broth, plus extra as required
- Salt and pepper

Directions:

1. Cook bacon in Dutch oven on moderate to high heat, stirring frequently, until crisp, approximately five minutes. Mix in onion and carrots and cook until vegetables start to become tender, approximately two minutes. Mix in garlic and thyme and cook until aromatic, approximately half a minute. Mix in tomatoes and bay leaf and cook until aromatic, approximately half a minute. Mix in lentils and ¼ teaspoon salt. Cover, decrease the heat to moderate to low, and cook until vegetables are softened and lentils have darkened, eight to ten minutes.
2. Increase heat to high, mix in wine, and bring to simmer. Mix in broth and water and bring to boil. Partially cover pot, decrease the heat to low, and simmer gently until lentils are tender but still hold their shape, 30 to 35 minutes.
3. Discard bay leaf. Process 3 cups soup using a blender until smooth, approximately half a minute, then return to pot. Heat soup gently over low heat until hot (do not boil) and adjust consistency with extra hot broth as required. Mix in vinegar and parsley and sprinkle with salt and pepper to taste. Serve.

Greek White Bean Soup

Yield: 6 Servings

Ingredients:

- 1 onion, chopped
- 1 pound (2½ cups) dried cannellini beans, picked over and rinsed
- 1 teaspoon ground dried Aleppo pepper
- 2 tablespoons chopped fresh parsley
- 2 tablespoons extra-virgin olive oil, plus extra for serving
- 2½ teaspoons minced fresh oregano or ¾ teaspoon dried
- 3 tablespoons lemon juice
- 4 celery ribs, cut into ½-inch pieces
- 6 cups chicken or vegetable broth, plus extra as required
- Salt and pepper

Directions:

1. Dissolve 3 tablespoons salt in 4 quarts cold water in large container. Put in beans and soak at room temperature for minimum 8 hours or for maximum 24 hours. Drain and wash thoroughly.
2. Heat oil in Dutch oven on moderate heat until it starts to shimmer. Put in onion, ½ teaspoon salt, and ½ teaspoon pepper and cook till they become tender and lightly browned, 5 to 7 minutes. Mix in oregano and cook until aromatic, approximately half a minute. Mix in broth, celery, and soaked beans and bring to boil. Decrease heat to low, cover, and simmer until beans are tender, 45 to 60 minutes.
3. Process 2 cups soup using a blender until smooth, approximately half a minute, then return to pot. Heat soup gently over low heat until hot (do not boil) and adjust consistency with extra hot broth as required. Mix in lemon juice, Aleppo, and parsley and sprinkle with salt and pepper to taste. Serve, drizzling individual portions with extra oil.

Green Pea Soup

Yield: 6 Servings

Ingredients:

QUICK PEA BROTH

- 1 carrot, chopped
- 1 garlic clove, lightly crushed
- 1 small onion, chopped
- 1 teaspoon salt
- 1¾ cups chicken broth
- 2 bay leaves
- 6 cups water
- 8 ounces snow peas, chopped

SOUP

- ½ cup dry white wine
- 1 cup Arborio rice
- 1 garlic clove, minced
- 1 onion, chopped fine
- 1½ ounces Parmesan cheese, grated (¾ cup)
- 2 ounces pancetta, chopped fine
- 2 tablespoons extra-virgin olive oil
- 2 teaspoons lemon juice
- 20 ounces frozen peas
- 4 teaspoons minced fresh parsley
- Salt and pepper

Directions:

1. FOR THE QUICK PEA BROTH Mix all ingredients in Dutch oven and bring to boil on moderate to high heat. Decrease heat to moderate to low, partially cover, and simmer for 30 minutes. Strain broth through fine-mesh strainer into moderate-sized saucepan, pressing on solids with wooden spoon to extract as much liquid as possible. Cover and keep warm over low heat until ready to use.
2. FOR THE SOUP Heat oil in now-empty pot on moderate heat until it starts to shimmer. Put in onion and pancetta and cook, stirring intermittently, until onion is softened and lightly browned, 5 to 7 minutes. Mix in garlic and cook until aromatic, approximately half a minute. Put in rice and cook, stirring often, until grain edges begin to turn translucent, approximately three minutes.
3. Put in wine and cook, stirring continuously, until fully absorbed, about 1 minute. Mix in warm broth and bring to boil. Decrease heat to moderate to low, cover, and simmer, stirring intermittently, until rice is just cooked, about fifteen minutes. Mix in peas and cook until heated through, approximately two minutes. Remove from the heat, mix in Parmesan, parsley, and lemon juice and sprinkle with salt and pepper to taste. Serve instantly.

Italian Pasta e Fagioli

Yield: 8 to 10 Servings

Ingredients:

- ¼ cup minced fresh parsley
- ¼ teaspoon red pepper flakes
- ½ teaspoon fennel seeds
- 1 (28-ounce) can diced tomatoes
- 1 celery rib, minced
- 1 cup orzo
- 1 fennel bulb, stalks discarded, bulb halved, cored, and chopped fine
- 1 onion, chopped fine
- 1 Parmesan cheese rind, plus grated Parmesan for serving
- 1 tablespoon extra-virgin olive oil, plus extra for serving
- 1 tablespoon minced fresh oregano or 1 teaspoon dried
- 2 (15-ounce) cans cannellini beans, rinsed
- 2 teaspoons grated orange zest
- 2½ cups water
- 3 anchovy fillets, rinsed and minced
- 3 ounces pancetta, chopped fine
- 3½ cups chicken broth
- 4 garlic cloves, minced
- Salt and pepper

Directions:

1. Heat oil in Dutch oven on moderate to high heat until it starts to shimmer. Put in pancetta and cook, stirring intermittently, until starting to brown, 3 to 5 minutes. Mix in onion, fennel, and celery and cook until vegetables are softened, 5 to 7 minutes. Mix in garlic, anchovies, oregano, orange zest, fennel seeds, and pepper flakes and cook until aromatic, about 1 minute.
2. Mix in tomatoes and their juice, scraping up any browned bits. Mix in Parmesan rind and beans, bring to simmer, and cook until flavours blend, about 10 minutes.
3. Mix in broth, water, and 1 teaspoon salt. Increase heat to high and bring to boil. Mix in pasta and cook until al dente, about 10 minutes. Remove from the heat, discard Parmesan rind. Mix in parsley and sprinkle with salt and pepper to taste. Serve, drizzling individual portions with extra oil and sprinkling with grated Parmesan.

Libyan Lamb-Mint Sharba

Yield: 6 to 8 Servings

Ingredients:

- ¼ teaspoon ground cumin
- ½ teaspoon ground cinnamon

- 1 (15-ounce) can chickpeas, rinsed
- 1 cup orzo
- 1 onion, chopped fine
- 1 pound lamb shoulder chops (blade or round bone), 1 to 1½ inches thick, trimmed and halved
- 1 tablespoon extra-virgin olive oil
- 1 teaspoon ground turmeric
- 1 teaspoon paprika
- 10 cups chicken broth
- 1½ teaspoons dried mint, crumbled
- 2 tablespoons tomato paste
- 4 plum tomatoes, cored and cut into ¼-inch pieces
- Salt and pepper

Directions:

1. Place oven rack to lower-middle position and pre-heat your oven to 325 degrees. Pat lamb dry using paper towels and sprinkle with salt and pepper. Heat oil in Dutch oven on moderate to high heat until just smoking. Brown lamb, about 4 minutes each side; move to plate. Pour off all but 2 tablespoons fat from pot.
2. Put in onion to fat left in pot and cook on moderate heat till they become tender, approximately five minutes. Mix in tomatoes and cook till they become tender and juice has evaporated, approximately two minutes. Mix in tomato paste, 1 teaspoon mint, turmeric, paprika, 1 teaspoon salt, cinnamon, cumin, and ¼ teaspoon pepper and cook until aromatic, about 1 minute. Mix in broth, scraping up any browned bits, and bring to boil.
3. Mix in chickpeas, then nestle lamb into pot along with any accumulated juices. Cover, place pot in oven, and cook until fork slips easily in and out of lamb, about 1 hour.
4. Move lamb to slicing board, allow to cool slightly, then shred into bite-size pieces using 2 forks, discarding excess fat and bones. In the meantime, stir orzo into soup, bring to simmer on moderate heat, and cook until tender, 10 to 12 minutes.
5. Mix in shredded lamb and cook until heated through, approximately two minutes. Remove from the heat, mix in remaining ½ teaspoon mint and allow to sit until aromatic, about 1 minute. Serve.

Moroccan Chickpea Soup

Yield: 4 to 6 Servings

Ingredients:

- ¼ cup minced fresh parsley or mint
- ¼ teaspoon ground cumin
- ¼ teaspoon ground ginger
- ¼ teaspoon saffron threads, crumbled
- ½ teaspoon hot paprika
- 1 (14.5-ounce) can diced tomatoes
- 1 onion, chopped fine

- 1 pound red potatoes, unpeeled, cut into ½-inch pieces
- 1 teaspoon sugar
- 1 zucchini, cut into ½-inch pieces
- 2 (15-ounce) cans chickpeas, rinsed
- 3 tablespoons extra-virgin olive oil
- 3½ cups chicken or vegetable broth
- 4 garlic cloves, minced
- Lemon wedges
- Salt and pepper

Directions:

1. Heat oil in Dutch oven on moderate to high heat until it starts to shimmer. Put in onion, sugar, and ½ teaspoon salt and cook until onion is softened, approximately five minutes. Mix in garlic, paprika, saffron, ginger, and cumin and cook until aromatic, approximately half a minute. Mix in chickpeas, potatoes, tomatoes and their juice, zucchini, and broth. Bring to simmer and cook, stirring intermittently, until potatoes are tender, 20 to 30 minutes.
2. Using wooden spoon, mash some of potatoes against side of pot to thicken soup. Remove from the heat, mix in parsley and sprinkle with salt and pepper to taste. Serve with lemon wedges.

Moroccan Spicy Fava Bean Soup

Yield: 4 to 6 Servings

Ingredients:

- ¼ cup lemon juice (2 lemons)
- 1 onion, chopped
- 1 pound (3 cups) dried split fava beans, picked over and rinsed
- 2 cups water
- 2 teaspoons cumin, plus extra for serving
- 2 teaspoons paprika, plus extra for serving
- 3 tablespoons extra-virgin olive oil, plus extra for serving
- 5 garlic cloves, minced
- 6 cups chicken or vegetable broth, plus extra as required
- Salt and pepper

Directions:

1. Heat oil in Dutch oven on moderate heat until it starts to shimmer. Put in onion, ¾ teaspoon salt, and ¼ teaspoon pepper and cook till they become tender and lightly browned, 5 to 7 minutes. Mix in garlic, paprika, and cumin and cook until aromatic, approximately half a minute.
2. Mix in beans, broth, and water and bring to boil. Cover, decrease the heat to low, and simmer gently, stirring intermittently, until beans are soft and broken down, 1½ to 2 hours.
3. Remove from the heat, beat soup heavily until broken down to coarse puree, approximately half a minute. Adjust consistency with extra hot broth as required. Mix in lemon juice and

sprinkle with salt and pepper to taste. Serve, drizzling individual portions with extra oil and sprinkling with extra paprika and cumin.

Provençal Vegetable Soup

Yield: 6 Servings

This is a timeless French soup made with seasonal vegetables, creamy white beans, and aromatic herbs.

Ingredients:

PISTOU

- ⅓ cup extra-virgin olive oil
- ½ cup fresh basil leaves
- 1 garlic clove, minced
- 1 ounce Parmesan cheese, grated (½ cup)

SOUP

- ½ cup orecchiette
- 1 (15-ounce) can cannellini or navy beans, rinsed
- 1 carrot, peeled and sliced ¼ inch thick
- 1 celery rib, cut into ½-inch pieces
- 1 large tomato, cored, seeded, and chopped
- 1 leek, white and light green parts only, halved along the length, sliced ½ inch thick, and washed thoroughly
- 1 small zucchini, halved along the length, seeded, and cut into ¼-inch pieces
- 1 tablespoon extra-virgin olive oil
- 2 garlic cloves, minced
- 3 cups vegetable broth
- 3 cups water
- 8 ounces haricots verts, trimmed and cut into ½-inch lengths
- Salt and pepper

Directions:

1. **For the Pistou** : Process all ingredients using a food processor until smooth, approximately fifteen seconds, scraping down sides of the container as required. (Pistou will keep safely in a fridge for maximum 4 hours.)
2. **For the Soup** : Heat oil in Dutch oven on moderate heat until it starts to shimmer. Put in leek, celery, carrot, and ½ teaspoon salt and cook until vegetables are softened, eight to ten minutes. Mix in garlic and cook until aromatic, approximately half a minute. Mix in broth and water and bring to simmer.
3. Mix in pasta and simmer until slightly softened, approximately five minutes. Mix in haricots verts and simmer until bright green but still crunchy, approximately three minutes. Mix in cannellini beans, zucchini, and tomato and simmer until pasta and vegetables are tender, approximately three minutes. Drizzle with salt and pepper to taste. Serve, topping individual portions with pistou.

Provene Fish Soup

Yield: 6 to 8 Servings

Ingredients:

- ⅛ teaspoon red pepper flakes
- 1 cup dry white wine or dry vermouth
- 1 fennel bulb, 2 tablespoons fronds minced, stalks discarded, bulb halved, cored, and cut into ½-inch pieces
- 1 onion, chopped
- 1 tablespoon extra-virgin olive oil, plus extra for serving
- 1 tablespoon grated orange zest
- 1 teaspoon paprika
- 2 (8-ounce) bottles clam juice
- 2 bay leaves
- 2 celery ribs, halved along the length and cut into ½-inch pieces
- 2 pounds skinless hake fillets, 1 to 1½ inches thick, sliced crosswise into 6 equivalent pieces
- 2 tablespoons minced fresh parsley
- 4 cups water
- 4 garlic cloves, minced
- 6 ounces pancetta, chopped fine
- Pinch saffron threads, crumbled
- Salt and pepper

Directions:

1. Heat oil in Dutch oven on moderate heat until it starts to shimmer. Put in pancetta and cook, stirring intermittently, until starting to brown, 3 to 5 minutes. Mix in fennel pieces, onion, celery, and 1½ teaspoons salt and cook until vegetables are softened and lightly browned, 12 to 14 minutes. Mix in garlic, paprika, pepper flakes, and saffron and cook until aromatic, approximately half a minute.
2. Mix in wine, scraping up any browned bits. Mix in water, clam juice, and bay leaves. Bring to simmer and cook until flavours blend, fifteen to twenty minutes.
3. Remove from the heat, discard bay leaves. Nestle hake into cooking liquid, cover, and allow to sit until fish flakes apart when softly poked using paring knife and registers 140 degrees, eight to ten minutes. Gently mix in parsley, fennel fronds, and orange zest and break fish into large pieces. Drizzle with salt and pepper to taste. Serve, drizzling individual portions with extra oil.

Red Pepper Roast Soup with Sides

Yield: 6 Servings

Roasted red peppers bring a rich smoky flavour to the soup.

Ingredients:

- ½ cup half-and-half

- ½ cup whole-milk yogurt
- ½ teaspoon ground cumin
- ½ teaspoon smoked paprika
- 1 bay leaf
- 1 red onion, chopped
- 1 tablespoon all-purpose flour
- 1 tablespoon extra-virgin olive oil
- 1 teaspoon lime juice
- 2 garlic cloves, minced
- 2 tablespoons dry sherry
- 2 tablespoons tomato paste
- 3 tablespoons minced fresh cilantro
- 4 cups chicken or vegetable broth, plus extra as required
- 8 red bell peppers, cored and flattened
- Salt and pepper

Directions:

1. Beat yogurt, 1 tablespoon cilantro, and lime juice together in a container. Drizzle with salt and pepper to taste. Cover and put in the fridge until needed.
2. Place oven rack 3 inches from broiler element and heat broiler. Lay out half of peppers skin side up on a baking sheet coated with an aluminium foil. Broil until skin is charred and puffed but flesh is still firm, eight to ten minutes, rotating sheet halfway through broiling. Move broiled peppers to a container, cover up using plastic wrap or foil, and let steam until skins peel off easily, 10 to fifteen minutes. Replicate the process with the rest of the peppers. Peel broiled peppers, discarding skins, and chop coarse.
3. Cook oil and garlic together in Dutch oven over low heat, stirring continuously, until garlic is foamy, sticky, and straw-colored, six to eight minutes. Mix in onion and ¼ teaspoon salt, increase heat to medium, and cook till they become tender, approximately five minutes.
4. Mix in cumin and paprika and cook until aromatic, approximately half a minute. Mix in tomato paste and flour and cook for about sixty seconds. Slowly beat in broth, scraping up any browned bits and smoothing out any lumps. Mix in bay leaf and chopped peppers, bring to simmer, and cook until peppers are very tender, 5 to 7 minutes.
5. Discard bay leaf. Working in batches, process soup using a blender until smooth, approximately two minutes. Return soup to clean pot and mix in half-and-half and sherry. Heat soup gently over low heat until hot (do not boil) and adjust consistency with extra hot broth as required. Mix in remaining 2 tablespoons cilantro and sprinkle with salt and pepper to taste. Serve, drizzling individual portions with yogurt mixture.

Shellfish Soup

Yield: 6 to 8 Servings

Ingredients:

- ⅛ teaspoon red pepper flakes
- ⅓ cup minced fresh parsley

- ½ teaspoon ground turmeric
- 1 cup dry white wine or dry vermouth
- 1 teaspoon grated fresh ginger
- 1 teaspoon ground coriander
- 1½ pounds leeks, white and light green parts only, halved along the length, sliced thin, and washed thoroughly
- 12 ounces large sea scallops, tendons removed
- 12 ounces large shrimp (26 to 30 per pound), peeled and deveined, shells reserved
- 12 ounces squid, bodies sliced crosswise into ½-inch-thick rings, tentacles halved
- 2 (8-ounce) bottles clam juice
- 2 garlic cloves, minced
- 2 tablespoons extra-virgin olive oil, plus extra for serving
- 3 tablespoons tomato paste
- 4 cups water
- 4 ounces pancetta, chopped fine
- Salt and pepper

Directions:

1. Heat 1 tablespoon oil in Dutch oven on moderate heat until it starts to shimmer. Put in shrimp shells and cook, stirring often, until starting to turn spotty brown and pot starts to brown, 2 to 4 minutes. Put in wine and simmer, stirring intermittently, for 2 minutes. Mix in water, bring to simmer, and cook for 4 minutes. Strain mixture through fine-mesh strainer into a container, pressing on solids to extract as much liquid as possible; discard solids.

2. Heat residual 1 tablespoon oil in now-empty pot on moderate heat until it starts to shimmer. Put in leeks and pancetta and cook until leeks are softened and lightly browned, approximately eight minutes. Mix in tomato paste, garlic, 1 teaspoon salt, ginger, coriander, turmeric, and pepper flakes and cook until aromatic, about 1 minute. Mix in wine mixture and clam juice, scraping up any browned bits. Bring to simmer and cook until flavours blend, fifteen to twenty minutes.

3. Decrease heat to gentle simmer, put in sea scallops, and cook for 2 minutes. Mix in shrimp and cook until just opaque throughout, approximately two minutes. Remove from the heat, mix in squid, cover, and allow to sit until just opaque and tender, 1 to 2 minutes. Mix in parsley and sprinkle with salt and pepper to taste. Serve, drizzling individual portions with extra oil.

Baba Ghanoush

Yield: Approximately 2 cups

Baba ghanoush is a delicious and nutritious meze staple popular in Israel, Lebanon, Palestine, and many other countries!

Ingredients:

- 1 small garlic clove, minced
- 2 eggplants (1 pound each), pricked all over with fork
- 2 tablespoons extra-virgin olive oil, plus extra for serving

- 2 tablespoons tahini
- 2 teaspoons chopped fresh parsley
- 4 teaspoons lemon juice
- Salt and pepper to taste

Directions:

1. Place the oven rack in the centre of the oven and pre-heat your oven to 500 degrees. Place eggplants on a baking sheet coated with aluminium foil and roast, flipping the eggplants every fifteen minutes, until consistently soft when pressed using tongs, forty minutes to one hour. Allow eggplants to cool for 5 minutes over a baking sheet.
2. Place a colander on top of a container. Slice the top and bottom off each eggplant and slit eggplants along the length. Using spoon, scoop hot pulp into colander (you should have about 2 cups pulp); discard skins. Allow the pulp to drain for about three minutes.
3. Move drained eggplant to your food processor. Put in tahini, oil, lemon juice, garlic, ¾ teaspoon salt, and ¼ teaspoon pepper. Pulse the mixture until a rough puree is achieved, approximately 8 pulses. Drizzle with salt and pepper to taste.
4. Move to serving bowl, cover firmly using plastic wrap, put inside your fridge until chilled, about 1 hour. (Dip will keep safely in a fridge for up to 24 hours; bring to room temperature before you serve.) Drizzle with salt and pepper to taste, sprinkle with extra oil to taste, and drizzle with parsley before you serve.

Brown Feta

Yield: 8 to 12 Servings

This vegetarian appetizer is for all the Feta lovers out there. Quick and easy to prepare, this recipe tastes great with parsley and olive oil.

Ingredients:

- 2 (8-ounce) blocks feta cheese, sliced into ½-inch-thick slabs
- ¼ teaspoon red pepper flakes
- ¼ teaspoon pepper
- 2 tablespoons extra-virgin olive oil
- 2 teaspoons minced fresh parsley

Directions:

1. Place oven rack 4 inches from broiler element and heat broiler. Pat feta dry using paper towels and lay out on broiler-safe gratin dish.
2. Drizzle with red pepper flakes and pepper. Broil until edges of cheese start to look golden, three to eight minutes. Sprinkle with oil, drizzle with parsley, and serve instantly.

Bruschetta with Artichoke Hearts and Parmesan

Yield: 8 to 10 Servings

Ingredients:

- 1 cup jarred whole baby artichoke hearts packed in water, rinsed and patted dry
- 1 garlic clove, minced
- 1 recipe Toasted Bread for Bruschetta
- 2 ounces Parmesan cheese, 1 ounce grated fine, 1 ounce shaved
- 2 tablespoons chopped fresh basil
- 2 tablespoons extra-virgin olive oil, plus extra for serving
- 2 teaspoons lemon juice
- Salt and pepper

Directions:

1. Pulse artichoke hearts, oil, basil, lemon juice, garlic, ¼ teaspoon salt, and ¼ teaspoon pepper using a food processor until coarsely pureed, about 6 pulses, scraping down sides of the container as required. Put in grated Parmesan and pulse to combine, about 2 pulses.
2. Lay out artichoke mixture uniformly toasts and top with shaved Parmesan. Season with pepper to taste, and sprinkle with extra oil to taste. Serve.

Bruschetta with Arugula Pesto and Goat Cheese

Yield: 8 to 10 Servings

Ingredients:

- ¼ cup extra-virgin olive oil, plus extra for serving
- ¼ cup pine nuts, toasted
- 1 recipe Toasted Bread for Bruschetta
- 1 tablespoon minced shallot
- 1 teaspoon grated lemon zest plus 1 teaspoon juice
- 2 ounces goat cheese, crumbled
- 5 ounces (5 cups) baby arugula
- Salt and pepper

Directions:

1. Pulse arugula, oil, pine nuts, shallot, lemon zest and juice, ½ teaspoon salt, and ¼ teaspoon pepper using a food processor until mostly smooth, approximately 8 pulses, scraping down sides of the container as required.
2. Lay out arugula mixture uniformly toasts, top with goat cheese, and sprinkle with extra oil to taste. Serve.

Bruschetta with Black Olive Pesto, Ricotta, and Basil

Yield: 8 to 10 Servings

Ingredients:

- ¾ cup pitted kalamata olives

- 1 garlic clove, minced
- 1 recipe Toasted Bread for Bruschetta
- 1 small shallot, minced
- 10 ounces whole-milk ricotta cheese
- 1½ teaspoons lemon juice
- 2 tablespoons extra-virgin olive oil, plus extra for serving
- 2 tablespoons shredded fresh basil
- Salt and pepper

Directions:

1. Pulse olives, shallot, oil, lemon juice, and garlic using a food processor until coarsely chopped, approximately ten pulses, scraping down sides of the container as required. Season ricotta with salt and pepper to taste.
2. Lay out ricotta mixture uniformly toasts, top with olive mixture, and sprinkle with extra oil to taste. Drizzle with basil before you serve.

Bruschetta with Ricotta, Tomatoes, and Basil

Yield: 8 to 10 Servings

Ingredients:

- 1 pound cherry tomatoes, quartered
- 1 recipe Toasted Bread for Bruschetta
- 1 tablespoon extra-virgin olive oil, plus extra for serving
- 10 ounces whole-milk ricotta cheese
- 5 tablespoons shredded fresh basil
- Salt and pepper

Directions:

1. Toss tomatoes with 1 teaspoon salt using a colander and allow to drain for about fifteen minutes. Move drained tomatoes to a container, toss with oil and ¼ cup basil, and sprinkle with salt and pepper to taste. In a different container, combine ricotta with remaining 1 tablespoon basil and sprinkle with salt and pepper to taste.
2. Lay out ricotta mixture uniformly toasts, top with tomato mixture, and drizzle lightly with extra oil to taste. Serve.

Caponata

Yield: Approximately 3 cups

A delicious and nutritious snack for all eggplant lovers!

Ingredients:

- ¼ cup chopped fresh parsley
- ¼ cup pine nuts, toasted

- ¼ cup raisins
- ¼ cup red wine vinegar, plus extra for seasoning
- ½ teaspoon salt
- ¾ cup V8 juice
- 1 celery rib, chopped fine
- 1 large eggplant (1½ pounds), cut into ½-inch cubes
- 1 large tomato, cored, seeded, and chopped
- 1 red bell pepper, stemmed, seeded, and chopped fine
- 1 small onion, chopped fine (½ cup)
- 1½ teaspoons minced anchovy fillets (2 to 3 fillets)
- 2 tablespoons brown sugar
- 2 tablespoons extra-virgin olive oil
- 2 tablespoons minced black olives

Directions:

1. Toss eggplant with salt in a container. Thoroughly coat the full surface of big microwave-safe plate using double layer of coffee filters and lightly spray using vegetable oil spray. Lay out eggplant in a uniform layer on coffee filters. Microwave until eggplant is dry and shriveled to one-third of its original size, about eight to fifteen minutes (Do not let it brown). Move eggplant instantly to paper towel–lined plate.
2. In the meantime, beat V8 juice, vinegar, sugar, parsley, and anchovies together in medium bowl. Mix in tomato, raisins, and olives.
3. Heat 1 tablespoon oil in 12-inch non-stick frying pan on moderate to high heat until it starts to shimmer. Put in eggplant and cook, stirring intermittently, until edges become browned, about four to eight minutes, adding 1 teaspoon more oil if pan seems to be dry; move to a container.
4. Put in remaining 2 teaspoons oil to now-empty frying pan and heat on moderate to high heat until it starts to shimmer. Put in celery, bell pepper, and onion and cook, stirring intermittently, till they become tender and edges are spotty brown, 6 to 8 minutes.
5. Decrease heat to moderate to low and mix in eggplant and V8 juice mixture. Bring to simmer and cook until V8 juice becomes thick and covers the vegetables, four to eight minutes. Move to serving bowl and allow to cool to room temperature. (Caponata will keep safely in a fridge for up to seven days; bring to room temperature before you serve.)
6. Drizzle with extra vinegar to taste and drizzle with pine nuts before you serve.

Classic Hummus

Yield: Approximately 2 cups

A popular recipe enjoyed throughout the eastern Mediterranean, Classic Hummus is an easy snack to prepare using simple ingredients!

Ingredients:

- ¼ cup water
- ¼ teaspoon ground cumin
- ½ teaspoon salt

- 1 (15-ounce) can chickpeas, rinsed
- 1 small garlic clove, minced
- 2 tablespoons extra-virgin olive oil, plus extra for serving
- 3 tablespoons lemon juice
- 6 tablespoons tahini
- Pinch cayenne pepper

Directions:

1. Mix water and lemon juice in a small-sized container. In a different container, beat tahini and oil together.
2. Process chickpeas, garlic, salt, cumin, and cayenne using a food processor until thoroughly ground, approximately fifteen seconds.
3. Scrape down sides of the container using a rubber spatula. While the machine runs, put in lemon juice mixture gradually. Scrape down sides of the container and carry on processing for about sixty seconds. While the machine runs, put in tahini mixture gradually and process until hummus is smooth and creamy, approximately fifteen seconds, scraping down sides of the container as required.
4. Move hummus to serving bowl, cover up using plastic wrap, and allow to sit at room temperature until flavours blend, approximately half an hour.
5. If you wish, you can refrigerate this dish for up to 5 days.
6. If needed, loosen hummus using 1 tablespoon warm water. Sprinkle with extra oil to taste before you serve.

Dolmathes

Yield: 24

A Greek delicacy, this recipe is basically stuffed grape leaves.

Ingredients:

- ¼ cup chopped fresh mint
- ⅓ cup chopped fresh dill
- ¾ cup short-grain white rice
- 1 (16-ounce) jar grape leaves
- 1 large onion, chopped fine
- 1½ tablespoons grated lemon zest plus 2 tablespoons juice
- 2 tablespoons extra-virgin olive oil, plus extra for serving
- Salt and pepper

Directions:

1. Reserve 24 intact grape leaves, approximately 6 inches in diameter; save for later rest of the leaves. Bring 6 cups water to boil in moderate-sized saucepan. Put in reserved grape leaves and cook for about sixty seconds. Gently drain leaves and move to a container of cold water to cool, about 5 minutes. Drain again, then move leaves to plate and cover loosely using plastic wrap.
2. Heat oil in now-empty saucepan over medium heat until it starts to shimmer. Put in onion and ½ teaspoon salt and cook till they become tender and lightly browned, 5 to 7 minutes.

Put in rice and cook, stirring frequently, until grain edges begin to turn translucent, approximately two minutes. Mix in ¾ cup water and bring to boil. Decrease heat to low, cover, and simmer gently until rice becomes soft but still firm in center and water has been absorbed, 10 to 12 minutes. Remove from the heat, let rice cool slightly, about 10 minutes. Mix in dill, mint, and lemon zest. (Blanched grape leaves and filling will keep safely in a fridge for up to 24 hours.)

3. Place 1 blanched leaf smooth side down on counter with stem facing you. Get rid of the stem from base of leaf by slicing along both sides of stem to form thin triangle. Pat leaf dry using paper towels. Overlap cut ends of leaf to stop any filling from leaking out. Place heaping tablespoon filling ¼ inch from bottom of leaf where ends overlap. Fold bottom over filling and fold in sides. Roll leaf tightly around filling to create tidy roll. Replicate the process with the rest of the blanched leaves and filling.

4. Line 12-inch frying pan with one layer of remaining leaves. Place rolled leaves seam side down in tight rows in prepared skillet. Mix 1¼ cups water and lemon juice, put in to skillet, and bring to simmer over medium heat. Cover, decrease the heat to moderate to low, and simmer until water is almost completely absorbed and leaves and rice are tender and cooked through, forty to sixty minutes.

5. Move stuffed grape leaves to serving platter and allow to cool to room temperature, approximately half an hour; discard leaves in skillet. Sprinkle with extra oil before you serve.

Easy Toasted Almonds

Yield: 2 cups

Meze platters are a delicious part of the Mediterranean diet, and toasted nuts are a vital part of it.

Ingredients:

- ¼ teaspoon pepper
- 1 tablespoon extra-virgin olive oil
- 1 teaspoon salt
- 2 cups skin-on raw whole almonds

Directions:

1. Heat oil in 12-inch non-stick frying pan on moderate to high heat until it barely starts shimmering. Put in almonds, salt, and pepper and decrease the heat to moderate to low. Cook, stirring frequently, until almonds become aromatic and their colour becomes somewhat deep, approximately eight minutes.
2. Move almonds to plate coated using paper towels and allow to cool before you serve.
3. If you wish, you can store Almonds at room temperature for up to 5 days.

Fiery Red Whipped Feta

Yield: Approximately 2 cups

The Greeks call this recipe "htipiti". This simple dish tastes great and is super quick and easy to make.

Ingredients:

- ¼ teaspoon pepper
- ⅓ cup extra-virgin olive oil, plus extra for serving
- ½ teaspoon cayenne pepper
- 1 cup jarred roasted red peppers, rinsed, patted dry, and chopped
- 1 tablespoon lemon juice
- 8 ounces feta cheese, crumbled (2 cups)

Directions:

1. Process feta, red peppers, oil, lemon juice, cayenne, and pepper using a food processor until smooth, approximately half a minute, scraping down sides of the container as required.
2. Move mixture to serving bowl, sprinkle with extra oil to taste, and serve. (Dip will keep safely in a fridge for up to 2 days; bring to room temperature before you serve.)

Flavourful Calamari with Oranges

Yield: 6 to 8 Servings

An aromatic snack from Fance!

Ingredients:

- ¼ cup extra-virgin olive oil
- ⅓ cup hazelnuts, toasted, skinned, and chopped
- 1 red bell pepper, stemmed, seeded, and cut into 2-inch-long matchsticks
- 1 shallot, sliced thin
- 1 teaspoon Dijon mustard
- 2 celery ribs, sliced thin on bias
- 2 garlic cloves, minced
- 2 oranges
- 2 pounds squid, bodies sliced crosswise into ¼-inch-thick rings, tentacles halved
- 2 tablespoons baking soda
- 2½ tablespoons harissa
- 3 tablespoons chopped fresh mint
- 3 tablespoons red wine vinegar
- Salt and pepper

Directions:

1. Dissolve baking soda and 1 tablespoon salt in 3 cups cold water in large container. Submerge squid in brine, cover, put inside your fridge for about fifteen minutes. Remove squid from brine and separate bodies from tentacles.
2. Bring 8 cups water to boil in a big saucepan on moderate to high heat. Fill big container with ice water. Put in 2 tablespoons salt and tentacles to boiling water and cook for 30 seconds. Put in bodies and cook until bodies are firm and opaque throughout, about 90 seconds. Drain squid, move to ice water, and allow to sit until chilled, about 5 minutes.
3. Beat oil, vinegar, harissa, garlic, mustard, 1½ teaspoons salt, and ½ teaspoon pepper together in a big container. Drain squid well and put in to a container with dressing.
4. Cut away peel and pith from oranges. Quarter oranges, then slice crosswise into ½-inch-thick pieces. Put in oranges, bell pepper, celery, and shallot to squid and toss to coat. Cover and

put in the fridge for minimum sixty minutes or up to 24 hours. Mix in hazelnuts and mint and sprinkle with salt and pepper to taste before you serve.

Sicilian Chickpea-Escarole Soup

Yield: 6 to 8 Servings

Ingredients:

- ¼ teaspoon red pepper flakes
- 1 (3-inch) strip orange zest
- 1 head escarole (1 pound), trimmed and cut into 1-inch pieces
- 1 large tomato, cored and chopped
- 1 Parmesan cheese rind, plus grated Parmesan for serving
- 1 pound (2¾ cups) dried chickpeas, picked over and rinsed
- 1 small onion, chopped
- 2 bay leaves
- 2 fennel bulbs, stalks discarded, bulbs halved, cored, and chopped fine
- 2 tablespoons extra-virgin olive oil, plus extra for serving
- 2 teaspoons minced fresh oregano or ½ teaspoon dried
- 5 cups chicken or vegetable broth
- 5 garlic cloves, minced
- Salt and pepper

Directions:

1. Dissolve 3 tablespoons salt in 4 quarts cold water in large container. Put in chickpeas and soak at room temperature for minimum 8 hours or for maximum 24 hours. Drain and wash thoroughly.
2. Heat oil in Dutch oven on moderate heat until it starts to shimmer. Put in fennel, onion, and 1 teaspoon salt and cook until vegetables are softened, 7 to 10 minutes. Mix in garlic, oregano, and pepper flakes and cook until aromatic, approximately half a minute.
3. Mix in 7 cups water, broth, soaked chickpeas, Parmesan rind, bay leaves, and orange zest and bring to boil. Reduce to gentle simmer and cook until chickpeas are tender, 1¼ to 1¾ hours.
4. Mix in escarole and tomato and cook until escarole is wilted, 5 to 10 minutes. Remove from the heat, discard bay leaves and Parmesan rind (scraping off any cheese that has melted and adding it back to pot). Drizzle with salt and pepper to taste. Serve, drizzling individual portions with extra oil and sprinkling with grated Parmesan.

Spanish Lentil-Chorizo Soup

Yield: 6 to 8 Servings

Ingredients:

- ⅛ teaspoon ground cloves
- 1 large onion
- 1 pound (2¼ cups) lentils, picked over and rinsed
- 1 tablespoon all-purpose flour

- 1½ pounds Spanish-style chorizo sausage, pricked with fork several times
- 2 bay leaves
- 2 tablespoons sweet smoked paprika
- 3 carrots, peeled and cut into ¼-inch pieces
- 3 garlic cloves, minced
- 3 tablespoons minced fresh parsley
- 3 tablespoons sherry vinegar, plus extra for seasoning
- 5 tablespoons extra-virgin olive oil
- Salt and pepper

Directions:

1. Place lentils and 2 teaspoons salt in heatproof container. Cover with 4 cups boiling water and let soak for 30 minutes. Drain well.

2. In the meantime, finely chop three-quarters of onion (you should have about 1 cup) and grate remaining quarter (you should have about 3 tablespoons). Heat 2 tablespoons oil in Dutch oven on moderate heat until it starts to shimmer. Put in chorizo and cook until browned on all sides, six to eight minutes. Move chorizo to large plate. Decrease heat to low and put in chopped onion, carrots, 1 tablespoon parsley, and 1 teaspoon salt. Cover and cook, stirring intermittently, until vegetables are very soft but not brown, 25 to 30 minutes. If vegetables begin to brown, put in 1 tablespoon water to pot.

3. Put in lentils and vinegar to vegetables, increase heat to medium-high, and cook, stirring often, until vinegar starts to evaporate, three to five minutes. Put in 7 cups water, chorizo, bay leaves, and cloves; bring to simmer. Decrease heat to low; cover; and cook until lentils are tender, approximately half an hour.

4. Heat remaining 3 tablespoons oil in small saucepan on moderate heat until it starts to shimmer. Put in paprika, grated onion, garlic, and ½ teaspoon pepper; cook, stirring continuously, until aromatic, 2 minutes. Put in flour and cook, stirring continuously, 1 minute longer. Remove chorizo and bay leaves from lentils. Stir paprika mixture into lentils and carry on cooking until flavors have blended and soup has thickened, 10 to fifteen minutes. When chorizo is cool enough to handle, cut in half along the length, then cut each half into ¼-inch-thick slices. Return chorizo to soup along with remaining 2 tablespoons parsley and heat through, about 1 minute. Drizzle with salt, pepper, and up to 2 teaspoons vinegar to taste and serve. (Soup can be made up to 3 days in advance.)

Spanish Meatball-Saffron Soup

Yield: 6 to 8 Servings

Ingredients:

MEATBALLS

- ⅓ cup whole milk
- ½ teaspoon pepper
- ½ teaspoon salt
- 1 ounce Manchego cheese, grated (½ cup)
- 1 shallot, minced

- 2 slices hearty white sandwich bread, torn into quarters
- 2 tablespoons extra-virgin olive oil
- 3 tablespoons minced fresh parsley
- 8 ounces 80 percent lean ground beef
- 8 ounces ground pork

SOUP

- ⅛ teaspoon red pepper flakes
- ¼ teaspoon saffron threads, crumbled
- 1 cup dry white wine
- 1 onion, chopped fine
- 1 recipe Picada
- 1 red bell pepper, stemmed, seeded, and cut into ¾-inch pieces
- 1 tablespoon extra-virgin olive oil
- 1 teaspoon paprika
- 2 garlic cloves, minced
- 2 tablespoons minced fresh parsley
- 8 cups chicken broth
- Salt and pepper

Directions:

1. FOR THE MEATBALLS Using fork, mash bread and milk together till it turns into a paste in a big container. Mix in ground pork, Manchego, parsley, shallot, oil, salt, and pepper until combined. Put in ground beef and knead with your hands until combined. Pinch off and roll 2-teaspoon-size pieces of mixture into balls and lay out on rimmed baking sheet (you should have 30 to 35 meatballs). Cover using plastic wrap put inside your fridge until firm, minimum 30 minutes.
2. FOR THE SOUP Heat oil in large Dutch oven on moderate to high heat until it starts to shimmer. Put in onion and bell pepper and cook till they become tender and lightly browned, eight to ten minutes. Mix in garlic, paprika, saffron, and pepper flakes and cook until aromatic, approximately half a minute. Mix in wine, scraping up any browned bits, and cook until almost completely evaporated, about 1 minute.
3. Mix in broth and bring to simmer. Gently put in meatballs and simmer until cooked through, 10 to 12 minutes. Remove from the heat, mix in picada and parsley and sprinkle with salt and pepper to taste. Serve.

Spicy Moroccan Lamb Lentil Soup

Yield: 6 to 8 Servings

Ingredients:

- ¼ cup harissa, plus extra for serving
- ¼ teaspoon cayenne pepper
- ¼ teaspoon ground cinnamon
- ⅓ cup minced fresh cilantro
- ½ teaspoon paprika

- ¾ cup green or brown lentils, picked over and rinsed
- 1 (15-ounce) can chickpeas, rinsed
- 1 onion, chopped fine
- 1 pound lamb shoulder chops (blade or round bone), 1 to 1½ inches thick, trimmed and halved
- 1 tablespoon all-purpose flour
- 1 tablespoon extra-virgin olive oil
- 1 teaspoon grated fresh ginger
- 1 teaspoon ground cumin
- 10 cups chicken broth
- 4 plum tomatoes, cored and cut into ¾-inch pieces
- Pinch saffron threads, crumbled
- Salt and pepper

Directions:

1. Place oven rack to lower-middle position and pre-heat your oven to 325 degrees. Pat lamb dry using paper towels and sprinkle with salt and pepper. Heat oil in Dutch oven on moderate to high heat until just smoking. Brown lamb, about 4 minutes each side; move to plate. Pour off all but 2 tablespoons fat from pot.
2. Put in onion to fat left in pot and cook on moderate heat till they become tender, approximately five minutes. Mix in ginger, cumin, paprika, cinnamon, cayenne, ¼ teaspoon pepper, and saffron and cook until aromatic, approximately half a minute. Mix in flour and cook for about sixty seconds. Slowly beat in broth, scraping up any browned bits and smoothing out any lumps, and bring to boil.
3. Nestle lamb into pot along with any accumulated juices, bring to simmer, and cook for about ten minutes. Mix in lentils and chickpeas, cover, and place pot in oven. Cook until fork slips easily in and out of lamb and lentils are tender, fifty to sixty minutes.
4. Move lamb to slicing board, allow to cool slightly, then shred into bite-size pieces using 2 forks, discarding excess fat and bones. Stir shredded lamb into soup and allow to sit until heated through, approximately two minutes. Mix in tomatoes, cilantro, and harissa and sprinkle with salt and pepper to taste. Serve, passing extra harissa separately.

Spicy Red Lentil Soup

Yield: 4 to 6 Servings

Ingredients:

- ⅛ teaspoon ground cinnamon
- ¼ cup chopped fresh cilantro
- ¼ cup extra-virgin olive oil
- ¼ teaspoon ground ginger
- ½ teaspoon ground cumin
- ¾ teaspoon ground coriander
- 1 garlic clove, minced
- 1 large onion, chopped fine

- 1 tablespoon tomato paste
- 1 teaspoon paprika
- 10½ ounces (1½ cups) red lentils, picked over and rinsed
- 1½ teaspoons dried mint, crumbled
- 2 cups water
- 2 tablespoons lemon juice, plus extra for seasoning
- 4 cups chicken or vegetable broth, plus extra as required
- Pinch cayenne pepper
- Salt and pepper

Directions:

1. Heat 2 tablespoons oil in a big saucepan on moderate heat until it starts to shimmer. Put in onion and 1 teaspoon salt and cook, stirring intermittently, till they become tender, approximately five minutes. Mix in coriander, cumin, ginger, cinnamon, ¼ teaspoon pepper, and cayenne and cook until aromatic, approximately two minutes. Mix in tomato paste and garlic and cook for about sixty seconds.
2. Mix in broth, water, and lentils and bring to vigorous simmer. Cook, stirring intermittently, until lentils are soft and about half are broken down, about fifteen minutes.
3. Beat soup heavily until broken down to coarse puree, approximately half a minute. Adjust consistency with extra hot broth as required. Mix in lemon juice and sprinkle with salt and extra lemon juice to taste. Cover and keep warm.
4. Heat remaining 2 tablespoons oil in small frying pan on moderate heat until it starts to shimmer. Remove from the heat, mix in mint and paprika. Serve soup, drizzling individual portions with 1 teaspoon spiced oil and sprinkling with cilantro.

Tomato Soup with Eggplant Roast

Yield: 4 to 6 Servings

Eastern Mediterranean countries love to couple tomatoes with eggplant!

Ingredients:

- ¼ cup raisins
- ½ teaspoon ground cumin
- 1 (14.5-ounce) can diced tomatoes, drained
- 1 bay leaf
- 1 onion, chopped
- 1½ teaspoons ras el hanout
- 2 garlic cloves, minced
- 2 pounds eggplant, cut into ½-inch pieces
- 2 tablespoons minced fresh cilantro
- 2 tablespoons slivered almonds, toasted
- 2 teaspoons lemon juice
- 4 cups chicken or vegetable broth, plus extra as required
- 6 tablespoons extra-virgin olive oil, plus extra for serving
- Salt and pepper

Directions:

1. Place oven rack 4 inches from broiler element and heat broiler. Toss eggplant with 5 tablespoons oil, then spread in aluminum foil–lined rimmed baking sheet. Broil eggplant for about ten minutes. Stir eggplant and continue to broil until mahogany brown, 5 to 7 minutes. Measure out and reserve 2 cups eggplant.

2. Heat residual 1 tablespoon oil in a big saucepan on moderate heat until it starts to shimmer. Put in onion, ¾ teaspoon salt, and ¼ teaspoon pepper and cook till they become tender and lightly browned, 5 to 7 minutes. Mix in garlic, ras el hanout, and cumin and cook until aromatic, approximately half a minute. Mix in broth, tomatoes, raisins, bay leaf, and remaining eggplant and bring to simmer. Decrease heat to low, cover, and simmer gently until eggplant is softened, approximately twenty minutes.

3. Discard bay leaf. Working in batches, process soup using a blender until smooth, approximately two minutes. Return soup to clean saucepan and mix in reserved eggplant. Heat soup gently over low heat until hot (do not boil) and adjust consistency with extra hot broth as required. Mix in lemon juice and sprinkle with salt and pepper to taste. Serve, sprinkling individual portions with almonds and cilantro and drizzling with extra oil.

Traditional Greek Avgolemono

Yield: 6 to 8 Servings

Ingredients:

- ½ cup long-grain white rice
- 1 bay leaf
- 1 scallion, sliced thin, or 3 tablespoons chopped fresh mint
- 1½ teaspoons salt
- 12 (4-inch) strips lemon zest plus ¼ cup juice (2 lemons)
- 2 large eggs plus 2 large yolks, room temperature
- 4 green cardamom pods, crushed, or 2 whole cloves
- 8 cups chicken broth

Directions:

1. Bring broth to boil in moderate-sized saucepan on high heat. Mix in rice, lemon zest, cardamom pods, bay leaf, and salt. Reduce to simmer and cook until rice becomes soft and broth is aromatic, 16 to 20 minutes.

2. Gently beat whole eggs, egg yolks, and lemon juice together in medium bowl until combined. Discard bay leaf, cardamom, and zest strips. Decrease heat to low. Whisking continuously, slowly ladle about 2 cups hot broth into egg mixture and beat until combined. Pour egg mixture back into saucepan and cook, stirring continuously, until soup is slightly thickened and wisps of steam appear, approximately five minutes (do not simmer or boil). Sprinkle individual portions with scallion and serve instantly.

Turkish Tomato Grain Soup

Yield: 6 to 8 Servings

A Turkish tomato soup empowered by flavourful grains!

Ingredients:

- ⅛ teaspoon red pepper flakes
- ⅓ cup chopped fresh mint
- ½ cup dry white wine
- ½ teaspoon smoked paprika
- ¾ cup medium-grind bulgur, rinsed
- 1 (28-ounce) can diced fire-roasted tomatoes
- 1 onion, chopped
- 1 tablespoon tomato paste
- 1 teaspoon dried mint, crumbled
- 2 cups water
- 2 red bell peppers, stemmed, seeded, and chopped
- 2 tablespoons extra-virgin olive oil
- 3 garlic cloves, minced
- 4 cups chicken or vegetable broth
- Salt and pepper

Directions:

1. Heat oil in Dutch oven on moderate heat until it starts to shimmer. Put in onion, bell peppers, ¾ teaspoon salt, and ¼ teaspoon pepper and cook till they become tender and lightly browned, six to eight minutes. Mix in garlic, dried mint, smoked paprika, and pepper flakes and cook until aromatic, approximately half a minute. Mix in tomato paste and cook for about sixty seconds.
2. Mix in wine, scraping up any browned bits, and simmer until reduced by half, about 1 minute. Put in tomatoes and their juice and cook, stirring intermittently, until tomatoes soften and begin to break apart, about 10 minutes.
3. Mix in broth, water, and bulgur and bring to simmer. Decrease heat to low, cover, and simmer gently until bulgur is tender, approximately twenty minutes. Drizzle with salt and pepper to taste. Serve, sprinkling individual portions with fresh mint.

Vegetable Broth Base

Yield: Approximately 1¾ cups base, or about 1¾ gallons broth

A quick, easy, and flavourful vegetable broth.

Ingredients:

- ½ cup (½ ounce) fresh parsley leaves and thin stems
- ½ small celery root, peeled and cut into ½-inch pieces (¾ cup)
- 1 pound leeks, white and light green parts only, chopped and washed (2½ cups)
- 1½ tablespoons tomato paste
- 2 carrots, peeled and cut into ½-inch pieces (⅔ cup)
- 3 tablespoons dried minced onion
- 3 tablespoons kosher salt

Directions:

1. Process leeks, carrots, celery root, parsley, dried minced onion, and salt using a food processor, pausing to scrape down sides of the container often, until paste is as fine as possible, three to five minutes. Put in tomato paste and process for 2 minutes, scraping down sides of the container every 30 seconds. Move mixture to airtight container and tap tightly on counter to eliminate air bubbles. Press small piece of parchment paper flush against surface of mixture and cover firmly. Freeze for maximum 6 months.
2. For each cup you wish to serve, stir 1 tablespoon fresh or frozen broth base into 1 cup boiling water. If particle-free broth is desired, allow broth to steep for about five minutes, then strain through fine-mesh strainer.

White Gazpacho

Yield: 6 to 8 Servings

A rich and elegant soup for when you want to impress!

Ingredients:

- ⅛ teaspoon almond extract
- ½ cup plus 2 teaspoons extra-virgin olive oil, plus extra for serving
- 1 garlic clove, peeled and smashed
- 2½ cups (8¾ ounces) plus ⅓ cup sliced blanched almonds
- 3 tablespoons sherry vinegar
- 4 cups water
- 6 ounces seedless green grapes, sliced thin (1 cup)
- 6 slices hearty white sandwich bread, crusts removed
- Pinch cayenne pepper
- Salt and pepper

Directions:

1. Mix bread and water in a container and let soak for about five minutes. Process 2½ cups almonds using a blender until finely ground, approximately half a minute, scraping down sides of blender jar as required. Using your hands, remove bread from water, squeeze it lightly, and move to blender with almonds. Measure out 3 cups soaking water and set aside; move remaining soaking water to blender. Put in garlic, vinegar, ½ teaspoon salt, and cayenne to blender and process until mixture has consistency of cake batter, 30 to 45 seconds. With blender running, put in ½ cup oil in thin, steady stream, approximately half a minute. Put in reserved soaking water and process for about sixty seconds.
2. Season soup with salt and pepper to taste, then strain through fine-mesh strainer into a container, pressing on solids to extract as much liquid as possible; discard solids.
3. Move 1 tablespoon soup to different container and mix in almond extract. Return 1 teaspoon extract-soup mixture to soup; discard remaining mixture. Cover and put in the fridge to combine the flavours, minimum 4 hours or for maximum 24 hours.
4. Heat remaining 2 teaspoons oil in 8-inch frying pan on moderate to high heat until it starts to shimmer. Put in remaining ⅓ cup almonds and cook, stirring continuously, until golden

brown, three to five minutes. Immediately move almonds to a container, mix in ¼ teaspoon salt, and allow to cool slightly.
5. Ladle soup into shallow bowls. Mound grapes in center of each bowl, drizzle with almonds, and drizzle with extra oil. Serve instantly.

Balsamic-Mustard Vinaigrette

Yield: ¼ cup

This is best for dressing assertive greens.

Ingredients:

- ⅛ teaspoon salt
- ½ teaspoon mayonnaise
- ½ teaspoon minced fresh thyme
- 1 tablespoon balsamic vinegar
- 1½ teaspoons minced shallot
- 2 teaspoons Dijon mustard
- 3 tablespoons extra-virgin olive oil
- Pinch pepper

Directions:

1. Beat vinegar, mustard, shallot, mayonnaise, thyme, salt, and pepper together in a container until smooth.
2. Whisking continuously, slowly drizzle in oil until completely blended. (Vinaigrette will keep safely in a fridge for maximum 2 weeks.)

Classic Vinaigrette

Yield: ¼ cup

This dressing works well with all types of greens.

Ingredients:

- ⅛ teaspoon salt
- ½ teaspoon Dijon mustard
- ½ teaspoon mayonnaise
- 1 tablespoon wine vinegar
- 1½ teaspoons minced shallot
- 3 tablespoons extra-virgin olive oil
- Pinch pepper

Directions:

1. Beat vinegar, shallot, mayonnaise, mustard, salt, and pepper together in a container until smooth.
2. Whisking continuously, slowly drizzle in oil until completely blended. (Vinaigrette will keep safely in a fridge for maximum 2 weeks.)

Herb Vinaigrette

Yield: ¼ cup

Serve this vinaigrette immediately.

Ingredients:

- ⅛ teaspoon salt
- ½ teaspoon Dijon mustard
- ½ teaspoon mayonnaise
- ½ teaspoon minced fresh thyme, tarragon, marjoram, or oregano
- 1 tablespoon minced fresh parsley or chives
- 1 tablespoon wine vinegar
- 1½ teaspoons minced shallot
- 3 tablespoons extra-virgin olive oil
- Pinch pepper

Directions:

1. Beat vinegar, parsley, shallot, thyme, mayonnaise, mustard, salt, and pepper together in a container until smooth.
2. Whisking continuously, slowly drizzle in oil until completely blended.

Lemon Vinaigrette

Yield: ¼ cup

This is best for dressing mild greens.

Ingredients:

- ⅛ teaspoon salt
- ¼ teaspoon grated lemon zest plus
- ½ teaspoon Dijon mustard
- ½ teaspoon mayonnaise
- 1 tablespoon juice
- 3 tablespoons extra-virgin olive oil
- Pinch pepper
- Pinch sugar

Directions:

1. Beat lemon zest and juice, mayonnaise, mustard, salt, pepper, and sugar together in a container until smooth.
2. Whisking continuously, slowly drizzle in oil until completely blended. (Vinaigrette will keep safely in a fridge for maximum 2 weeks.)

Tahini-Lemon Dressing

Yield: Approximately ½ cup

Ingredients:

- ⅛ teaspoon pepper
- ¼ cup extra-virgin olive oil
- ½ teaspoon salt
- 1 garlic clove, minced
- 1 tablespoon water
- 2 tablespoons tahini
- 2½ tablespoons lemon juice

Directions:

1. Beat lemon juice, tahini, water, garlic, salt, and pepper together in a container until smooth.
2. Whisking continuously, slowly drizzle in oil until completely blended. (Dressing will keep safely in a fridge for maximum seven days.)

Walnut Vinaigrette

Yield: ¼ cup

Ingredients:

- ⅛ teaspoon salt
- ½ teaspoon Dijon mustard
- ½ teaspoon mayonnaise
- 1 tablespoon wine vinegar
- 1½ tablespoons extra-virgin olive oil
- 1½ tablespoons roasted walnut oil
- 1½ teaspoons minced shallot
- Pinch pepper

Directions:

1. Beat vinegar, shallot, mayonnaise, mustard, salt, and pepper together in a container until smooth.
2. Whisking continuously, slowly drizzle in oils until completely blended. (Vinaigrette will keep safely in a fridge for maximum 2 weeks.)

Green Salads

Salads are a vital component of the Mediterranean diet. Enjoy these with a dressing of your choice!

Arugula Fennel Parmesan Salad

Yield: 4 to 6 Servings

Ingredients:

- ¼ cup extra-virgin olive oil
- 1 large fennel bulb, stalks discarded, bulb halved, cored, and sliced thin
- 1 ounce Parmesan cheese, shaved

- 1 small garlic clove, minced
- 1 small shallot, minced
- 1 teaspoon Dijon mustard
- 1 teaspoon minced fresh thyme
- 1½ tablespoons lemon juice
- 6 ounces (6 cups) baby arugula
- Salt and pepper

Directions:

1. Gently toss arugula and fennel together in a big container. Beat lemon juice, shallot, mustard, thyme, garlic, ⅛ teaspoon salt, and pinch pepper together in a small-sized container.
2. Whisking continuously, slowly drizzle in oil. Sprinkle dressing over salad and gently toss to coat. Sprinkle with salt and pepper to taste. Serve, topping individual portions with Parmesan.

Arugula Mix Salad

Yield: 6 Servings

Ingredients:

- ¼ cup extra-virgin olive oil
- ½ cup dried figs, stemmed and chopped
- ½ cup walnuts, toasted and chopped
- 1 small shallot, minced
- 1 tablespoon raspberry jam
- 2 ounces Parmesan cheese, shaved
- 2 ounces thinly sliced prosciutto, cut into ¼-inch-wide ribbons
- 3 tablespoons balsamic vinegar
- 8 ounces (8 cups) baby arugula
- Salt and pepper

Directions:

1. Heat 1 tablespoon oil in 10-inch non-stick frying pan on moderate heat. Put in prosciutto and cook, stirring frequently, until crisp, approximately seven minutes. Use a slotted spoon to move prosciutto to paper towel–lined plate; set aside.
2. Beat vinegar, jam, shallot, ¼ teaspoon salt, and ⅛ teaspoon pepper together in a big container. Mix in figs, cover, and microwave until steaming, about 1 minute. Whisking continuously, slowly drizzle in remaining 3 tablespoons oil. Allow to sit until figs are softened and vinaigrette has cooled to room temperature, about fifteen minutes.
3. Just before you serve, beat vinaigrette to re-emulsify. Put in arugula and gently toss to coat. Sprinkle with salt and pepper to taste. Serve, topping individual portions with prosciutto, walnuts, and Parmesan.

Arugula Sweet Salad

Yield: 6 Servings

Honey can be substituted for the apricot jam.

Ingredients:

- ¼ small red onion, sliced thin
- ⅓ cup sliced almonds, toasted
- ½ cup dried apricots, chopped
- 1 ripe but firm pear, halved, cored, and sliced ¼ inch thick
- 1 small shallot, minced
- 1 tablespoon apricot jam
- 3 ounces goat cheese, crumbled (¾ cup)
- 3 tablespoons extra-virgin olive oil
- 3 tablespoons white wine vinegar
- 8 ounces (8 cups) baby arugula
- Salt and pepper

Directions:

1. Beat vinegar, jam, shallot, ¼ teaspoon salt, and ⅛ teaspoon pepper together in a big container. Put in apricots, cover, and microwave until steaming, about 1 minute. Whisking continuously, slowly drizzle in oil. Mix in onion and allow to sit until figs are softened and vinaigrette has cooled to room temperature, about fifteen minutes.
2. Just before you serve, beat vinaigrette to re-emulsify. Put in arugula and pear and gently toss to coat. Sprinkle with salt and pepper to taste. Serve, topping individual portions with almonds and goat cheese.

Asparagus Arugula Cannellini Salad

Yield: 4 to 6 Servings

Ingredients:

- ½ red onion, sliced thin
- 1 (15-ounce) can cannellini beans, rinsed
- 1 pound asparagus, trimmed and cut on bias into 1-inch lengths
- 2 tablespoons plus 2 teaspoons balsamic vinegar
- 5 tablespoons extra-virgin olive oil
- 6 ounces (6 cups) baby arugula
- Salt and pepper

Directions:

1. Heat 2 tablespoons oil in 12-inch non-stick frying pan on high heat until just smoking. Put in onion and cook until lightly browned, about 1 minute. Put in asparagus, ¼ teaspoon salt, and ¼ teaspoon pepper and cook, stirring intermittently, until asparagus is browned and crisp-tender, about 4 minutes. Move to a container, mix in beans, and allow to cool slightly.
2. Beat vinegar, ¼ teaspoon salt, and ⅛ teaspoon pepper together in a small-sized container. Whisking continuously, slowly drizzle in remaining 3 tablespoons oil. Gently toss arugula with 2 tablespoons dressing until coated. Sprinkle with salt and pepper to taste. Divide

arugula among plates. Toss asparagus mixture with remaining dressing, arrange over arugula, and serve.

Asparagus-Red Pepper-Spinach-Goat Cheese Salad

Yield: 4 to 6 Servings

Ingredients:

- 1 garlic clove, minced
- 1 pound asparagus, trimmed and cut on bias into 1-inch lengths
- 1 red bell pepper, stemmed, seeded, and cut into 2-inch-long matchsticks
- 1 shallot, halved and sliced thin
- 1 tablespoon plus 1 teaspoon sherry vinegar
- 2 ounces goat cheese, crumbled (½ cup)
- 5 tablespoons extra-virgin olive oil
- 6 ounces (6 cups) baby spinach
- Salt and pepper

Directions:

1. Heat 1 tablespoon oil in 12-inch non-stick frying pan on high heat until just smoking. Put in bell pepper and cook until lightly browned, approximately two minutes. Put in asparagus, ¼ teaspoon salt, and ⅛ teaspoon pepper and cook, stirring intermittently, until asparagus is browned and almost tender, approximately two minutes. Mix in shallot and cook till they become tender and asparagus is crisp-tender, about 1 minute. Move to a container and allow to cool slightly.
2. Beat vinegar, garlic, ¼ teaspoon salt, and ⅛ teaspoon pepper together in a small-sized container. Whisking continuously, slowly drizzle in remaining ¼ cup oil. Gently toss spinach with 2 tablespoons dressing until coated. Sprinkle with salt and pepper to taste. Divide spinach among plates. Toss asparagus mixture with remaining dressing and arrange over spinach. Sprinkle with goat cheese and serve.

Bitter Greens Olive Feta Salad

Yield: 4 to 6 Servings

Ingredients:

- ⅓ cup chopped fresh dill
- ⅓ cup pepperoncini, seeded and cut into ¼-inch-thick strips
- ½ cup pitted kalamata olives, halved
- 1 garlic clove, minced
- 1 head escarole (1 pound), trimmed and cut into 1-inch pieces
- 1 small head frisée (4 ounces), trimmed and torn into 1-inch pieces
- 2 ounces feta cheese, crumbled (½ cup)
- 2 tablespoons lemon juice

- 3 tablespoons extra-virgin olive oil
- Salt and pepper

Directions:

1. Gently toss escarole, frisée, olives, feta, and pepperoncini together in a big container. Beat dill, lemon juice, garlic, ¼ teaspoon salt, and ⅛ teaspoon pepper together in a small-sized container.
2. Whisking continuously, slowly drizzle in oil. Sprinkle dressing over salad and gently toss to coat. Serve.

Fiery Tuna-Olive Salad

Yield: 4 to 6 Servings

Ingredients:

- ½ cup pimento-stuffed green olives, chopped
- 1 (15-ounce) can cannellini beans, rinsed
- 1 garlic clove, minced
- 1 tablespoon chopped fresh parsley
- 12 ounces cherry tomatoes, halved
- 2 (12-ounce) tuna steaks, 1 to 1¼ inches thick
- 3 tablespoons lemon juice
- 5 ounces (5 cups) baby arugula
- 6 tablespoons extra-virgin olive oil
- Salt and pepper

Directions:

1. Beat olives, lemon juice, parsley, and garlic together in a big container. Whisking continuously, slowly drizzle in 5 tablespoons oil. Sprinkle with salt and pepper to taste.
2. Pat tuna dry using paper towels and sprinkle with salt and pepper. Heat residual 1 tablespoon oil in 12-inch non-stick frying pan on moderate to high heat until just smoking. Cook tuna until thoroughly browned and translucent red at center when checked with tip of paring knife and registers 110 degrees (for rare), approximately two minutes each side. Move to slicing board and slice into ½-inch-thick slices.
3. Beat dressing to re-emulsify, then drizzle 1 tablespoon dressing over tuna. Put in arugula, tomatoes, and beans to a container with remaining dressing and gently toss to combine. Sprinkle with salt and pepper to taste. Divide salad among plates and top with tuna. Serve.

Fundamental Green Salad

Yield: 4 Servings

Ingredients:

- ½ garlic clove, peeled
- 8 ounces (8 cups) lettuce, torn into bite-size pieces if needed
- Extra-virgin olive oil
- Salt and pepper

- Vinegar

Directions:

1. Take a salad bowl and coat its inside with garlic. Put in lettuce. Cautiously sprinkle lettuce with a little oil. Slowly toss the contents of the bowl. Carry on drizzling with oil and toss gently until greens are mildly coated and barely starting to shine.
2. Drizzle with small amounts of vinegar, salt, and pepper to taste and toss gently to coat. Serve.

Green Artichoke Olive Salad

Yield: 4 to 6 Servings

Ingredients:

- ⅓ cup fresh parsley leaves
- ⅓ cup pitted kalamata olives, halved
- 1 cup jarred whole baby artichoke hearts packed in water, quartered, rinsed, and patted dry
- 1 ounce Asiago cheese, shaved
- 1 romaine lettuce heart (6 ounces), cut into 1-inch pieces
- 1 small garlic clove, minced
- 2 tablespoons white wine vinegar or white balsamic vinegar
- 3 ounces (3 cups) baby arugula
- 3 tablespoons extra-virgin olive oil
- Salt and pepper

Directions:

1. Gently toss romaine, arugula, artichoke hearts, parsley, and olives together in a big container. Beat vinegar, garlic, ¼ teaspoon salt, and pinch pepper together in a small-sized container.
2. Whisking continuously, slowly drizzle in oil. Sprinkle vinaigrette over salad and gently toss to coat. Sprinkle with salt and pepper to taste. Serve, topping individual portions with Asiago.

Green Marcona Manchego Salad

Yield: 4 to 6 Servings

Ingredients:

- ¼ cup extra-virgin olive oil
- ⅓ cup Marcona almonds, chopped coarse
- 1 shallot, minced
- 1 teaspoon Dijon mustard
- 2 ounces Manchego cheese, shaved
- 5 teaspoons sherry vinegar
- 6 ounces (6 cups) mesclun greens
- Salt and pepper

Directions:

1. Place mesclun in a big container. Beat vinegar, shallot, mustard, ¼ teaspoon salt, and ¼ teaspoon pepper together in a small-sized container. Whisking continuously, slowly drizzle in oil.
2. Sprinkle vinaigrette over mesclun and gently toss to coat. Sprinkle with salt and pepper to taste. Serve, topping individual portions with almonds and Manchego.

Kale-Sweet Potato Salad

Yield: 6 to 8 Servings

Ingredients:

SALAD

- ⅓ cup pecans, toasted and chopped
- ½ head radicchio (5 ounces), cored and sliced thin
- 1½ pounds sweet potatoes, peeled, cut into ½-inch pieces
- 12 ounces Tuscan kale, stemmed and sliced crosswise into ½-inch-wide strips (7 cups)
- 2 teaspoons extra-virgin olive oil
- Salt and pepper
- Shaved Parmesan cheese

VINAIGRETTE

- ¼ cup extra-virgin olive oil
- 1 small shallot, minced
- 1 tablespoon cider vinegar
- 1 tablespoon honey
- 1½ tablespoons pomegranate molasses
- 2 tablespoons water
- Salt and pepper

Directions:

1. **For the Salad:** Place the oven rack in the centre of the oven and pre-heat your oven to 400 degrees. Toss sweet potatoes with oil and sprinkle with salt and pepper. Arrange potatoes in one layer in rimmed baking sheet and roast until browned, 25 to 30 minutes, flipping potatoes halfway through roasting. Move to plate and allow to cool for 20 minutes. In the meantime, heavily squeeze and massage kale with hands until leaves are uniformly darkened and slightly wilted, about 1 minute.
2. **For the Vinaigrette** : Beat water, pomegranate molasses, shallot, honey, vinegar, ¼ teaspoon salt, and ¼ teaspoon pepper together in a big container. Whisking continuously, slowly drizzle in oil.
3. Put in potatoes, kale, and radicchio to vinaigrette and gently toss to coat. Sprinkle with salt and pepper to taste. Move to serving platter and drizzle with pecans and shaved Parmesan to taste. Serve.

Mâche-Cucumber-Mint Salad

Yield: 6 to 8 Servings

Ingredients:

- ¼ cup extra-virgin olive oil
- ⅓ cup pine nuts, toasted
- ½ cup chopped fresh mint
- 1 cucumber, sliced thin
- 1 garlic clove, minced
- 1 tablespoon capers, rinsed and minced
- 1 tablespoon lemon juice
- 1 tablespoon minced fresh parsley
- 1 teaspoon minced fresh thyme
- 12 ounces (12 cups) mâche
- Salt and pepper

Directions:

1. Gently toss mâche, cucumber, mint, and pine nuts together in a big container. Beat lemon juice, parsley, capers, thyme, garlic, ¼ teaspoon salt, and ¼ teaspoon pepper together in a small-sized container.
2. Whisking continuously, slowly drizzle in oil. Sprinkle dressing over salad and gently toss to coat. Sprinkle with salt and pepper to taste. Serve.

Salade Niçoise

Yield: 6 Servings

Ingredients:

DRESSING

- ¼ cup lemon juice (2 lemons)
- ¼ teaspoon pepper
- ½ cup extra-virgin olive oil
- ½ teaspoon salt
- 1 shallot, minced
- 1 teaspoon Dijon mustard
- 2 tablespoons minced fresh basil
- 2 teaspoons minced fresh oregano
- 2 teaspoons minced fresh thyme

SALAD

- ¼ cup pitted niçoise olives
- 1 small red onion, sliced thin
- 10–12 anchovy fillets, rinsed (optional)
- 1¼ pounds small red potatoes, unpeeled, quartered
- 2 (5-ounce) cans solid white tuna in water, drained and flaked
- 2 heads Boston lettuce or Bibb lettuce (1 pound), torn into bite-size pieces
- 2 tablespoons capers, rinsed (optional)
- 2 tablespoons dry vermouth

- 3 hard-cooked large eggs, peeled and quartered
- 3 small tomatoes, cored and cut into ½-inch-thick wedges
- 8 ounces green beans, trimmed and halved
- Salt and pepper

Directions:

1. **FOR THE DRESSING** : Beat lemon juice, shallot, basil, thyme, oregano, mustard, salt, and pepper together in a small-sized container. Whisking continuously, slowly drizzle in oil.
2. **FOR THE SALAD** : Place potatoes in a big saucepan, put in water to cover by 1 inch, and bring to boil on high heat. Put in 1 tablespoon salt, reduce to simmer, and cook until potatoes are soft and paring knife can be slipped in and out of potatoes with little resistance, 5 to 8 minutes. With slotted spoon, gently move potatoes to a container (do not discard water). Toss warm potatoes with ¼ cup vinaigrette and vermouth. Sprinkle with salt and pepper to taste; set aside.
3. As potatoes cook, mildly toss lettuce with ¼ cup vinaigrette in a container until coated. Arrange bed of lettuce on very large, flat serving platter. Place tuna in now-empty bowl and break up using a fork. Put in ¼ cup vinaigrette and stir to combine. Mound tuna in center of lettuce. In now-empty bowl, toss tomatoes and red onion with 2 tablespoons vinaigrette and sprinkle with salt and pepper to taste. Arrange tomato-onion mixture in mound at edge of lettuce bed. Arrange rest of the potatoes in separate mound at edge of lettuce bed.
4. Return water to boil and put in 1 tablespoon salt and green beans. Cook until crisp-tender, 3 to 5 minutes. In the meantime, fill big container halfway with ice and water. Drain green beans, move to ice water, and allow to sit until just cool, approximately half a minute. Move beans to triple layer of paper towels and dry well. In now-empty bowl, toss green beans with remaining 2 tablespoons vinaigrette and sprinkle with salt and pepper to taste. Arrange in separate mound at edge of lettuce bed.
5. Place eggs, olives, and anchovies, if using, in separate mounds at edge of lettuce bed. Sprinkle the whole salad with capers, if using. Serve.

Spinach-Feta-Pistachio Salad

Yield: 6 Servings

Ingredients:

- 1 (2-inch) strip lemon zest plus 1½ tablespoons juice
- 1 shallot, minced
- 10 ounces curly-leaf spinach, stemmed and torn into bite-size pieces
- 1½ ounces feta cheese, crumbled (⅓ cup)
- 2 teaspoons sugar
- 3 tablespoons chopped toasted pistachios
- 3 tablespoons extra-virgin olive oil
- 6 radishes, trimmed and sliced thin
- Salt and pepper

Directions:

1. Place feta on plate and freeze until mildly stiff, about fifteen minutes.

2. Cook oil, lemon zest, shallot, and sugar in Dutch oven over moderate to low heat until shallot is softened, approximately five minutes. Remove from the heat, discard zest and mix in lemon juice. Put in spinach, cover, and let steam off heat until it just begins to wilt, approximately half a minute.
3. Move spinach mixture and liquid left in pot to big container. Put in radishes, pistachios, and chilled feta and toss to combine. Sprinkle with salt and pepper to taste. Serve.

Tangy Salad

Yield: 4 to 6 Servings

Ingredients:

- ½ cup smoked almonds, chopped coarse
- ⅔ cup chopped pitted dates
- 1 small head radicchio (6 ounces), cored and sliced thin
- 1 small shallot, minced
- 1 teaspoon Dijon mustard
- 1 teaspoon sugar
- 2 red grapefruits
- 3 oranges
- 3 tablespoons extra-virgin olive oil
- Salt and pepper

Directions:

1. Cut away peel and pith from grapefruits and oranges. Cut each fruit in half from pole to pole, then slice crosswise ¼ inch thick. Move to a container, toss with sugar and ½ teaspoon salt, and allow to sit for about fifteen minutes.
2. Drain fruit in fine-mesh strainer set over bowl, reserving 2 tablespoons juice. Arrange fruit on serving platter and drizzle with oil. Beat reserved juice, shallot, and mustard together in medium bowl. Put in radicchio, ⅓ cup dates, and ¼ cup almonds and gently toss to coat. Sprinkle with salt and pepper to taste. Arrange radicchio mixture over fruit, leaving 1-inch border of fruit around edges. Sprinkle with remaining ⅓ cup dates and remaining ¼ cup almonds. Serve.

Tri-Balsamic Salad

Yield: 4 to 6 Servings

Ingredients:

- 1 head Belgian endive (4 ounces), cut into 2-inch pieces
- 1 small head radicchio (6 ounces), cored and cut into 1-inch pieces
- 1 tablespoon balsamic vinegar
- 1 teaspoon red wine vinegar
- 3 ounces (3 cups) baby arugula
- 3 tablespoons extra-virgin olive oil
- Salt and pepper

Directions:

1. Gently toss radicchio, endive, and arugula together in a big container. Beat balsamic vinegar, red wine vinegar, ⅛ teaspoon salt, and pinch pepper together in a small-sized container.
2. Whisking continuously, slowly drizzle in oil. Drizzle vinaigrette over salad and gently toss to coat. Drizzle with salt and pepper to taste. Serve.

Vegetable Salads

Algerian Mix Salad

Yield: 4 to 6 Servings

Ingredients:

- ¼ cup coarsely chopped fresh mint
- ¼ cup extra-virgin olive oil
- ½ cup pitted oil-cured black olives, quartered
- 2 fennel bulbs, stalks discarded, bulbs halved, cored, and sliced thin
- 2 tablespoons lemon juice
- 4 blood oranges
- Salt and pepper

Directions:

1. Cut away peel and pith from oranges. Quarter oranges, then slice crosswise into ¼-inch-thick pieces. Mix oranges, fennel, olives, and mint in a big container.
2. Beat lemon juice, ¼ teaspoon salt, and ⅛ teaspoon pepper together in a small-sized container. Whisking continuously, slowly drizzle in oil. Sprinkle dressing over salad and gently toss to coat. Sprinkle with salt and pepper to taste. Serve.

Asparagus Mix Salad

Yield: 4 to 6 Servings

Ingredients:

PESTO

- ¼ cup fresh basil leaves
- ¼ cup grated Pecorino Romano cheese
- ½ cup extra-virgin olive oil
- 1 garlic clove, minced
- 1 teaspoon grated lemon zest plus 2 teaspoons juice
- 2 cups fresh mint leaves
- Salt and pepper

SALAD

- ¾ cup hazelnuts, toasted, skinned, and chopped
- 2 oranges

- 2 pounds asparagus, trimmed
- 4 ounces feta cheese, crumbled (1 cup)
- Salt and pepper

Directions:

1. **For the Pesto:** Process mint, basil, Pecorino, lemon zest and juice, garlic, and ¾ teaspoon salt using a food processor until finely chopped, approximately half a minute, scraping down sides of the container as required. Move to big container. Mix in oil and sprinkle with salt and pepper to taste.
2. **For the Salad:** Chop asparagus tips from stalks into ¾-inch-long pieces. Cut asparagus stalks ⅛ inch thick on bias into approximate 2-inch lengths. Cut away the peel and pith from oranges. Holding fruit over bowl, use paring knife to cut between membranes to release segments. Put in asparagus tips and stalks, orange segments, feta, and hazelnuts to pesto and toss to combine. Sprinkle with salt and pepper to taste. Serve.

Scorched Beet Almond Salad

Yield: 4 to 6 Servings

Ingredients:

- 2 blood oranges
- 2 ounces (2 cups) baby arugula
- 2 ounces ricotta salata cheese, shaved
- 2 pounds beets, trimmed
- 2 tablespoons extra-virgin olive oil
- 2 tablespoons sliced almonds, toasted
- 4 teaspoons sherry vinegar
- Salt and pepper

Directions:

1. Place the oven rack in the centre of the oven and pre-heat your oven to 400 degrees. Wrap each beet individually in aluminium foil and place in rimmed baking sheet. Roast beets until it is easy to skewer the centre of beets with foil removed, forty minutes to one hour.
2. Cautiously open foil packets and allow beets to sit until cool enough to handle. Cautiously rub off beet skins using a paper towel. Slice beets into ½-inch-thick wedges, and, if large, cut in half crosswise.
3. Beat vinegar, ¼ teaspoon salt, and ¼ teaspoon pepper together in a big container. Whisking continuously, slowly drizzle in oil. Put in beets, toss to coat, and allow to cool to room temperature, approximately twenty minutes.
4. Cut away peel and pith from oranges. Quarter oranges, then slice crosswise into ½-inch-thick pieces. Put in oranges and arugula to a container with beets and gently toss to coat. Sprinkle with salt and pepper to taste. Move to serving platter and drizzle with ricotta salata and almonds. Serve.

Sweet Nut Winter Squash Salad

Yield: 4 to 6 Servings

Ingredients:

- ¼ cup extra-virgin olive oil
- ⅓ cup roasted, unsalted pepitas
- ½ cup pomegranate seeds
- ¾ cup fresh parsley leaves
- 1 small shallot, minced
- 1 teaspoon za'atar
- 2 tablespoons honey
- 2 tablespoons lemon juice
- 3 pounds butternut squash, peeled, seeded, and cut into ½-inch pieces (8 cups)
- Salt and pepper

Directions:

1. Place oven rack to lowest position and pre-heat your oven to 450 degrees. Toss squash with 1 tablespoon oil and sprinkle with salt and pepper. Arrange squash in one layer in rimmed baking sheet and roast until thoroughly browned and tender, 30 to 35 minutes, stirring halfway through roasting. Sprinkle squash with za'atar and allow to cool for about fifteen minutes.
2. Beat shallot, lemon juice, honey, and ¼ teaspoon salt together in a big container. Whisking continuously, slowly drizzle in remaining 3 tablespoons oil. Put in squash, parsley, and pepitas and gently toss to coat. Arrange salad on serving platter and drizzle with pomegranate seeds. Serve.

Tomato Mix Salad

Yield: 6 Servings

Ingredients:

- ¼ cup plain Greek yogurt
- 1 garlic clove, minced
- 1 scallion, sliced thin
- 1 tablespoon extra-virgin olive oil
- 1 tablespoon lemon juice
- 1 tablespoon minced fresh oregano
- 1 teaspoon ground cumin
- 2½ pounds ripe tomatoes, cored and cut into ½-inch-thick wedges
- 3 ounces feta cheese, crumbled (¾ cup)
- Salt and pepper

Directions:

1. Toss tomatoes with ½ teaspoon salt and allow to drain using a colander set over bowl for fifteen to twenty minutes.
2. Microwave oil, garlic, and cumin in a container until aromatic, approximately half a minute; allow to cool slightly. Move 1 tablespoon tomato liquid to big container; discard remaining

liquid. Beat in yogurt, lemon juice, scallion, oregano, and oil mixture until combined. Put in tomatoes and feta and gently toss to coat. Sprinkle with salt and pepper to taste. Serve.

Tomato-Burrata Mix Salad

Yield: 4 to 6 Servings

Ingredients:

- ½ cup chopped fresh basil
- 1 garlic clove, minced
- 1 shallot, halved and sliced thin
- 1½ pounds ripe tomatoes, cored and cut into 1-inch pieces
- 1½ tablespoons white balsamic vinegar
- 3 ounces rustic Italian bread, cut into 1-inch pieces (1 cup)
- 6 tablespoons extra-virgin olive oil
- 8 ounces burrata cheese, room temperature
- 8 ounces ripe cherry tomatoes, halved
- Salt and pepper

Directions:

1. Toss tomatoes with ¼ teaspoon salt and allow to drain using a colander for 30 minutes.
2. Pulse bread using a food processor into large crumbs measuring between ⅛ and ¼ inch, approximately ten pulses. Mix crumbs, 2 tablespoons oil, pinch salt, and pinch pepper in 12-inch non-stick skillet. Cook on moderate heat, stirring frequently, until crumbs are crisp and golden, about 10 minutes. Clear center of skillet, put in garlic, and cook, mashing it into skillet, until aromatic, approximately half a minute. Stir garlic into crumbs. Move to plate and allow to cool slightly.
3. Beat shallot, vinegar, and ¼ teaspoon salt together in a big container. Whisking continuously, slowly drizzle in remaining ¼ cup oil. Put in tomatoes and basil and gently toss to combine. Sprinkle with salt and pepper to taste and arrange on serving platter. Cut buratta into 1-inch pieces, collecting creamy liquid. Sprinkle burrata over tomatoes and drizzle with creamy liquid. Sprinkle with bread crumbs and serve instantly.

Tomato-Tuna Mix Salad

Yield: 6 Servings

Ingredients:

- ¼ cup capers, rinsed and minced
- ¼ cup extra-virgin olive oil
- ¼ cup finely chopped red onion
- ⅓ cup pitted kalamata olives, chopped coarse
- 1 (5-ounce) can solid white tuna in water, drained and flaked
- 1 tablespoon lemon juice
- 2 tablespoons chopped fresh parsley
- 2½ pounds ripe tomatoes, cored and cut into ½-inch-thick wedges

- Salt and pepper

Directions:

1. Toss tomatoes with ½ teaspoon salt and allow to drain using a colander set over bowl for fifteen to twenty minutes.
2. Move 1 tablespoon tomato liquid to big container; discard remaining liquid. Beat in oil, olives, capers, onion, parsley, and lemon juice until combined. Put in tomatoes and tuna and gently toss to coat. Sprinkle with salt and pepper to taste. Serve.

Yogurt-Mint Cucumber Salad

Yield: 4 Servings

Ingredients:

- ¼ cup minced fresh mint
- ½ teaspoon ground cumin
- 1 cup plain low-fat yogurt
- 1 garlic clove, minced
- 1 small red onion, sliced thin
- 2 tablespoons extra-virgin olive oil
- 3 cucumbers, peeled, halved along the length, seeded, and sliced ¼ inch thick
- Salt and pepper

Directions:

1. Toss cucumbers and onion with 1 tablespoon salt using a colander set over big container. Weight cucumber-onion mixture with 1 gallon-size zipper-lock bag filled with water; drain for 1 to three hours. Wash and pat dry.
2. Beat yogurt, mint, oil, garlic, and cumin together in a big container. Put in cucumber-onion mixture and toss to coat. Sprinkle with salt and pepper to taste. Serve at room temperature or chilled within one hour.

Zucchini Parmesan Salad

Yield: 6 to 8 Servings

Ingredients:

- ¼ cup lemon juice (2 lemons)
- ½ cup extra-virgin olive oil
- 1½ pounds small zucchini, trimmed and sliced along the length into ribbons
- 2 tablespoons minced fresh mint
- 6 ounces Parmesan cheese, shaved
- Salt and pepper

Directions:

1. Gently toss zucchini with salt and pepper to taste, then arrange beautifully on serving platter.
2. Sprinkle with oil and lemon juice, then drizzle with Parmesan and mint. Serve instantly.

Brussels Pecorino Pine Salad

Yield: 4 to 6 Servings

Ingredients:

- ¼ cup extra-virgin olive oil
- ¼ cup pine nuts, toasted
- 1 garlic clove, minced
- 1 pound Brussels sprouts, trimmed, halved, and sliced very thin
- 1 small shallot, minced
- 1 tablespoon Dijon mustard
- 2 ounces Pecorino Romano cheese, shredded (⅔ cup)
- 2 tablespoons lemon juice
- Salt and pepper

Directions:

1. Beat lemon juice, mustard, shallot, garlic, and ½ teaspoon salt together in a big container. Whisking continuously, slowly drizzle in oil. Put in Brussels sprouts, toss to coat, and allow to sit for minimum half an hour or maximum 2 hours.
2. Mix in Pecorino and pine nuts. Sprinkle with salt and pepper to taste. Serve.

Cauliflower Chermoula Salad

Yield: 4 to 6 Servings

Ingredients:

SALAD

- ½ cup raisins
- ½ red onion, sliced ¼ inch thick
- 1 cup shredded carrot
- 1 head cauliflower (2 pounds), cored and cut into 2-inch florets
- 2 tablespoons chopped fresh cilantro
- 2 tablespoons extra-virgin olive oil
- 2 tablespoons sliced almonds, toasted
- Salt and pepper

CHERMOULA

- ⅛ teaspoon cayenne pepper
- ¼ cup extra-virgin olive oil
- ¼ teaspoon salt
- ½ teaspoon ground cumin
- ½ teaspoon paprika
- ¾ cup fresh cilantro leaves
- 2 tablespoons lemon juice
- 4 garlic cloves, minced

Directions:

1. **For the Salad:** Place oven rack to lowest position and pre-heat your oven to 475 degrees. Toss cauliflower with oil and sprinkle with salt and pepper. Arrange cauliflower in one layer in parchment paper–lined rimmed baking sheet. Cover tightly with aluminium foil and roast till they become tender, 5 to 7 minutes. Remove foil and spread onion evenly in sheet. Roast until vegetables are tender, cauliflower becomes deeply golden brown, and onion slices are charred at edges, 10 to fifteen minutes, stirring halfway through roasting. Allow it to cool slightly, approximately five minutes.
2. **For the Chermoula:** Process all ingredients using a food processor until smooth, about 1 minute, scraping down sides of the container as required. Move to big container.
3. Gently toss cauliflower-onion mixture, carrot, raisins, and cilantro with chermoula until coated. Move to serving platter and drizzle with almonds. Serve warm or at room temperature.

Cherry Tomato Mix Salad

Yield: 4 to 6 Servings

Ingredients:

- ½ cup pitted kalamata olives, chopped
- ½ teaspoon sugar
- 1 shallot, minced
- 1 small cucumber, peeled, halved along the length, seeded, and cut into ½-inch pieces
- 1 tablespoon red wine vinegar
- 1½ pounds cherry tomatoes, quartered
- 2 garlic cloves, minced
- 2 tablespoons extra-virgin olive oil
- 2 teaspoons minced fresh oregano
- 3 tablespoons chopped fresh parsley
- 4 ounces feta cheese, crumbled (1 cup)
- Salt and pepper

Directions:

1. Toss tomatoes with sugar and ¼ teaspoon salt in a container and allow to sit for 30 minutes. Move tomatoes to salad spinner and spin until seeds and excess liquid have been removed, 45 to 60 seconds, stopping to redistribute tomatoes several times during spinning. Put in tomatoes, cucumber, olives, feta, and parsley to big container; set aside.
2. Strain ½ cup tomato liquid through fine-mesh strainer into liquid measuring cup; discard remaining liquid. Bring tomato liquid, shallot, vinegar, garlic, and oregano to simmer in small saucepan on moderate heat and cook until reduced to 3 tablespoons, six to eight minutes. Move to small-sized container and allow to cool to room temperature, approximately five minutes. Whisking continuously, slowly drizzle in oil. Sprinkle dressing over salad and gently toss to coat. Sprinkle with salt and pepper to taste. Serve.

Classic Greek Salad

Yield: 6 to 8 Servings

Ingredients:

- ¼ cup chopped fresh mint
- ¼ cup chopped fresh parsley
- ½ cup pitted kalamata olives, quartered
- ½ red onion, sliced thin
- 1 cup jarred roasted red peppers, rinsed, patted dry, and cut into ½-inch strips
- 1 garlic clove, minced
- 1 teaspoon lemon juice
- 1½ tablespoons red wine vinegar
- 2 cucumbers, peeled, halved along the length, seeded, and sliced thin
- 2 teaspoons minced fresh oregano
- 5 ounces feta cheese, crumbled (1¼ cups)
- 6 large ripe tomatoes, cored, seeded, and cut into ½-inch-thick wedges
- 6 tablespoons extra-virgin olive oil
- Salt and pepper

Directions:

1. Beat oil, vinegar, oregano, lemon juice, garlic, ½ teaspoon salt, and ⅛ teaspoon pepper together in a big container. Put in cucumbers and onion, toss to coat, and allow to sit for 20 minutes.
2. Put in tomatoes, red peppers, olives, parsley, and mint to a container with cucumber-onion mixture and toss to combine. Sprinkle with salt and pepper to taste. Move salad to wide, shallow serving bowl or platter and drizzle with feta. Serve instantly.

Crunchy Mushroom Salad

Yield: 6 Servings

Ingredients:

- ¼ cup extra-virgin olive oil
- ½ cup fresh parsley leaves
- 1 shallot, halved and sliced thin
- 1½ tablespoons lemon juice
- 2 ounces Parmesan cheese, shaved
- 2 tablespoons chopped fresh tarragon
- 4 celery ribs, sliced thin, plus ½ cup celery leaves
- 8 ounces cremini mushrooms, trimmed and sliced thin
- Salt and pepper

Directions:

1. Beat oil, lemon juice, and ¼ teaspoon salt together in a big container. Put in mushrooms and shallot, toss to coat, and allow to sit for about ten minutes.

2. Put in sliced celery and leaves, Parmesan, parsley, and tarragon to mushroom-shallot mixture and toss to combine. Sprinkle with salt and pepper to taste. Serve.

Cucumber Sesame-Lemon Salad

Yield: 4 Servings

Ingredients:

- ⅛ teaspoon red pepper flakes, plus extra for seasoning
- ¼ cup rice vinegar
- 1 tablespoon lemon juice
- 1 tablespoon sesame seeds, toasted
- 2 tablespoons toasted sesame oil
- 2 teaspoons sugar
- 3 cucumbers, peeled, halved along the length, seeded, and sliced ¼ inch thick
- Salt and pepper

Directions:

1. Toss cucumbers with 1 tablespoon salt using a colander set over big container. Weight cucumbers with 1 gallon-size zipper-lock bag filled with water; drain for 1 to three hours. Wash and pat dry.
2. Beat vinegar, oil, lemon juice, sesame seeds, sugar, and pepper flakes together in a big container. Put in cucumbers and toss to coat. Sprinkle with salt and pepper to taste. Serve at room temperature or chilled.

Cut Up Salad

Yield: 4 Servings

Ingredients:

- ½ cup chopped fresh parsley
- ½ cup pitted kalamata olives, chopped
- ½ small red onion, chopped fine
- 1 (15-ounce) can chickpeas, rinsed
- 1 cucumber, peeled, halved along the length, seeded, and cut into ½-inch pieces
- 1 garlic clove, minced
- 1 romaine lettuce heart (6 ounces), cut into ½-inch pieces
- 10 ounces grape tomatoes, quartered
- 3 tablespoons extra-virgin olive oil
- 3 tablespoons red wine vinegar
- 4 ounces feta cheese, crumbled (1 cup)
- Salt and pepper

Directions:

1. Toss cucumber and tomatoes with 1 teaspoon salt and allow to drain using a colander for about fifteen minutes.

2. Beat vinegar and garlic together in a big container. Whisking continuously, slowly drizzle in oil. Put in cucumber-tomato mixture, chickpeas, olives, onion, and parsley and toss to coat. Allow to sit for minimum 5 minutes or maximum 20 minutes.
3. Put in lettuce and feta and gently toss to combine. Sprinkle with salt and pepper to taste. Serve.

Fattoush

Yield: 4 to 6 Servings

Ingredients:

- ¼ teaspoon minced garlic
- ½ cup chopped fresh cilantro
- ½ cup chopped fresh mint
- 1 cup arugula, chopped coarse
- 1 English cucumber, peeled and sliced ⅛ inch thick
- 1 pound ripe tomatoes, cored and cut into ¾-inch pieces
- 2 (8-inch) pita breads
- 3 tablespoons lemon juice
- 4 scallions, sliced thin
- 4 teaspoons ground sumac, plus extra for sprinkling
- 7 tablespoons extra-virgin olive oil
- Salt and pepper

Directions:

1. Place the oven rack in the centre of the oven and pre-heat your oven to 375 degrees. Using kitchen shears, slice around perimeter of each pita and divide into 2 thin rounds. Cut each round in half. Place pitas smooth side down on wire rack set in rimmed baking sheet. Brush 3 tablespoons oil on surface of pitas. (Pitas do not need to be uniformly coated. Oil will spread during baking.) Sprinkle with salt and pepper. Bake until pitas are crisp and pale golden brown, 10 to 14 minutes. Allow it to cool to room temperature.
2. Beat lemon juice, sumac, garlic, and ¼ teaspoon salt together in a small-sized container and allow to sit for about ten minutes. Whisking continuously, slowly drizzle in remaining ¼ cup oil.
3. Break pitas into ½-inch pieces and place in a big container. Put in tomatoes, cucumber, arugula, cilantro, mint, and scallions. Sprinkle dressing over salad and gently toss to coat. Sprinkle with salt and pepper to taste. Serve, sprinkling individual portions with extra sumac.

French Potato Dijon Herb Salad

Yield: 4 to 6 Servings

Ingredients:

- ¼ cup extra-virgin olive oil
- ½ teaspoon pepper
- 1 garlic clove, peeled and threaded on skewer

- 1 small shallot, minced
- 1 tablespoon minced fresh chervil
- 1 tablespoon minced fresh chives
- 1 tablespoon minced fresh parsley
- 1 teaspoon minced fresh tarragon
- 1½ tablespoons white wine vinegar or Champagne vinegar
- 2 pounds small red potatoes, unpeeled, sliced ¼ inch thick
- 2 tablespoons salt
- 2 teaspoons Dijon mustard

Directions:

1. Place potatoes in a big saucepan, put in water to cover by 1 inch, and bring to boil on high heat. Put in salt, decrease the heat to simmer, and cook until potatoes are soft and paring knife can be slipped in and out of potatoes with little resistance, about 6 minutes.
2. While potatoes are cooking, lower skewered garlic into simmering water and blanch for 45 seconds. Run garlic under cold running water, then remove from skewer and mince.
3. Reserve ¼ cup cooking water, then drain potatoes and lay out on tight one layer in rimmed baking sheet. Beat oil, minced garlic, vinegar, mustard, pepper, and reserved potato cooking water together in a container, then drizzle over potatoes. Let potatoes sit until flavours blend, about 10 minutes. (Potatoes will keep safely in a fridge for maximum 8 hours; return to room temperature before you serve.)
4. Move potatoes to big container. Mix shallot and herbs in a small-sized container, then drizzle over potatoes and gently toss to coat using rubber spatula. Serve.

Green Bean Cilantro Salad

Yield: 6 to 8 Servings

Ingredients:

- ¼ cup walnuts
- ½ cup extra-virgin olive oil
- 1 scallion, sliced thin
- 2 garlic cloves, unpeeled
- 2 pounds green beans, trimmed
- 2½ cups fresh cilantro leaves and stems, tough stem ends trimmed (about 2 bunches)
- 4 teaspoons lemon juice
- Salt and pepper

Directions:

1. Cook walnuts and garlic in 8-inch frying pan on moderate heat, stirring frequently, until toasted and aromatic, 5 to 7 minutes; move to a container. Let garlic cool slightly, then peel and approximately chop.
2. Process walnuts, garlic, cilantro, oil, lemon juice, scallion, ½ teaspoon salt, and ⅛ teaspoon pepper using a food processor until smooth, about 1 minute, scraping down sides of the container as required; move to big container.

3. Bring 4 quarts water to boil in large pot on high heat. In the meantime, fill big container halfway with ice and water. Put in 1 tablespoon salt and green beans to boiling water and cook until crisp-tender, 3 to 5 minutes. Drain green beans, move to ice water, and allow to sit until chilled, approximately two minutes. Move green beans to a container with cilantro sauce and gently toss until coated. Sprinkle with salt and pepper to taste. Serve. (Salad will keep safely in a fridge for maximum 4 hours.)

Halloumi-Veg Salad

Yield: 4 to 6 Servings

Ingredients:

- ¼ cup extra-virgin olive oil
- ½ teaspoon grated lemon zest plus 3 tablespoons juice
- 1 (8-ounce) block halloumi cheese, sliced into ½-inch-thick slabs
- 1 garlic clove, minced
- 1 head radicchio (10 ounces), quartered
- 1 pound eggplant, sliced into ½-inch-thick rounds
- 1 tablespoon minced fresh thyme
- 1 zucchini, halved along the length
- 3 tablespoons honey
- Salt and pepper

Directions:

1. Beat honey, thyme, lemon zest and juice, garlic, ⅛ teaspoon salt, and ⅛ teaspoon pepper together in a big container; set aside. Brush eggplant, radicchio, zucchini, and halloumi with 2 tablespoons oil and sprinkle with salt and pepper.
2. **FOR A CHARCOAL GRILL:** Open bottom vent fully. Light large chimney starter half filled with charcoal briquettes (3 quarts). When top coals are partially covered with ash, pour uniformly over grill. Set cooking grate in place, cover, and open lid vent fully. Heat grill until hot, approximately five minutes.
3. **FOR A GAS GRILL:** Turn all burners to high, cover, and heat grill until hot, about fifteen minutes. Turn all burners to medium.
4. Clean cooking grate, then repetitively brush grate with thoroughly oiled paper towels until grate is black and glossy, 5 to 10 times. Place vegetables and cheese on grill. Cook (covered if using gas), flipping as required, until radicchio becomes tender and mildly charred, 3 to 5 minutes, and remaining vegetables and cheese are softened and mildly charred, about 10 minutes. Move vegetables and cheese to slicing board as they finish cooking, allow to cool slightly, then cut into 1-inch pieces.
5. Whisking continuously, slowly drizzle remaining 2 tablespoons oil into honey mixture. Put in vegetables and cheese and gently toss to coat. Sprinkle with salt and pepper to taste. Serve.

Italian Panzanella Mix Salad

Yield: 6 Servings

Ingredients:

- 1 (15-ounce) can cannellini beans, rinsed
- 1 small red onion, halved and sliced thin
- 1½ pounds ripe tomatoes, cored and chopped, seeds and juice reserved
- 12 ounces rustic Italian bread, cut into 1-inch pieces (4 cups)
- 2 ounces Parmesan cheese, shaved
- 2 tablespoons minced fresh oregano
- 3 ounces (3 cups) baby arugula
- 3 tablespoons chopped fresh basil
- 3 tablespoons red wine vinegar
- 5 tablespoons extra-virgin olive oil
- Salt and pepper

Directions:

1. Place the oven rack in the centre of the oven and pre-heat your oven to 350 degrees. Toss bread pieces with 1 tablespoon oil and sprinkle with salt and pepper. Arrange bread in one layer in rimmed baking sheet and bake, stirring intermittently, until light golden brown, fifteen to twenty minutes. Allow it to cool to room temperature.
2. Beat vinegar and ¼ teaspoon salt together in a big container. Whisking continuously, slowly drizzle in remaining ¼ cup oil. Put in tomatoes with their seeds and juice, beans, onion, 1½ tablespoons basil, and 1 tablespoon oregano, toss to coat, and allow to sit for 20 minutes.
3. Put in cooled croutons, arugula, remaining 1½ tablespoons basil, and remaining 1 tablespoon oregano and gently toss to combine. Sprinkle with salt and pepper to taste. Move salad to serving platter and drizzle with Parmesan. Serve.

Mackerel-Fennel-Apple Salad

Yield: 4 to 6 Servings

Ingredients:

- ¼ cup extra-virgin olive oil
- 1 fennel bulb, stalks discarded, bulb halved, cored, and sliced thin
- 1 small shallot, minced
- 1 tablespoon whole-grain mustard
- 2 Granny Smith apples, peeled, cored, and cut into 3-inch-long matchsticks
- 2 teaspoons minced fresh tarragon
- 3 tablespoons lemon juice
- 5 ounces (5 cups) watercress
- 6 ounces smoked mackerel, skin and pin bones removed, flaked
- Salt and pepper

Directions:

1. Beat lemon juice, mustard, shallot, 1 teaspoon tarragon, ½ teaspoon salt, and ¼ teaspoon pepper together in a big container. Whisking continuously, slowly drizzle in oil. Put in watercress, apples, and fennel and gently toss to coat. Sprinkle with salt and pepper to taste.
2. Divide salad among plates and top with flaked mackerel. Sprinkle any remaining dressing over mackerel and drizzle with remaining 1 teaspoon tarragon. Serve instantly.

Moroccan Carrot Salad

Yield: 4 to 6 Servings

Ingredients:

- ⅛ teaspoon cayenne pepper
- ⅛ teaspoon ground cinnamon
- ¾ teaspoon ground cumin
- 1 pound carrots, peeled and shredded
- 1 tablespoon lemon juice
- 1 teaspoon honey
- 2 oranges
- 3 tablespoons extra-virgin olive oil
- 3 tablespoons minced fresh cilantro
- Salt and pepper

Directions:

1. Cut away peel and pith from oranges. Holding fruit over bowl, use paring knife to slice between membranes to release segments. Cut segments in half crosswise and allow to drain in fine-mesh strainer set over big container, reserving juice.
2. Beat lemon juice, honey, cumin, cayenne, cinnamon, and ½ teaspoon salt into reserved orange juice. Put in drained oranges and carrots and gently toss to coat. Allow to sit until liquid starts to pool in bottom of bowl, 3 to 5 minutes.
3. Drain salad in fine-mesh strainer and return to now-empty bowl. Mix in cilantro and oil and sprinkle with salt and pepper to taste. Serve.

Radish-Fava Salad

Yield: 4 to 6 Servings

Ingredients:

- ¼ cup chopped fresh basil
- ¼ cup extra-virgin olive oil
- ¼ teaspoon ground coriander
- ¼ teaspoon pepper
- ½ teaspoon salt
- 10 radishes, trimmed, halved, and sliced thin
- 1½ ounces (1½ cups) pea shoots
- 2 garlic cloves, minced
- 3 pounds fava beans, shelled (3 cups)
- 3 tablespoons lemon juice

Directions:

1. Bring 4 quarts water to boil in large pot on high heat. In the meantime, fill big container halfway with ice and water. Put in fava beans to boiling water and cook for about sixty seconds. Drain fava beans, move to ice water, and allow to sit until chilled, approximately

two minutes. Move fava beans to triple layer of paper towels and dry well. Use a pairing knife to make small cut along edge of each bean through waxy sheath, then gently squeeze sheath to release bean; discard sheath.

2. Beat lemon juice, garlic, salt, pepper, and coriander together in a big container. Whisking continuously, slowly drizzle in oil. Put in fava beans, radishes, pea shoots, and basil and gently toss to coat. Serve instantly.

Roasted Beet-Carrot Salad with

Yield: 4 to 6 Servings

Ingredients:

- ½ cup shelled pistachios, toasted and chopped
- ½ teaspoon ground cumin
- 1 pound beets, trimmed
- 1 pound carrots, peeled and sliced on bias ¼ inch thick
- 1 small shallot, minced
- 1 tablespoon grated lemon zest plus 3 tablespoons juice
- 1 teaspoon honey
- 2 tablespoons minced fresh parsley
- 2½ tablespoons extra-virgin olive oil
- Salt and pepper

Directions:

1. Adjust oven racks to middle and lowest positions. Place rimmed baking sheet on lower rack and pre-heat your oven to 450 degrees.
2. Wrap each beet individually in aluminium foil and place in second rimmed baking sheet. Toss carrots with 1 tablespoon oil, ½ teaspoon salt, and ½ teaspoon pepper.
3. Quickly, arrange carrots in one layer in hot baking sheet and place baking sheet with beets on middle rack. Roast until carrots are soft and thoroughly browned on 1 side, 20 minutes to half an hour, and skewer can be inserted easily into the center of the beets with aluminium foil removed 35 to 45 minutes.
4. Cautiously open foil packets and allow beets to sit until cool enough to handle. Cautiously rub off beet skins using paper towel. Slice beets into ½-inch-thick wedges, and, if large, cut in half crosswise.
5. Beat lemon juice, shallot, honey, cumin, ¼ teaspoon salt, and ⅛ teaspoon pepper together in a big container. Whisking continuously, slowly drizzle in remaining 1½ tablespoons oil. Put in beets and carrots, toss to coat, and allow to cool to room temperature, approximately twenty minutes.
6. Put in pistachios, parsley, and lemon zest to a container with beets and carrots and toss to coat. Sprinkle with salt and pepper to taste. Serve.

Made in the USA
Las Vegas, NV
22 June 2025

23922158R00033